Education, Culture, Individualism

Public School in a Struggle for Authority

J. D. Stewart

Dedication:

To my wife, Barbara, and my former teaching colleagues who have rolled the Sisyphysean rock of public education up hill day after day for decades.

Table Of Contents

It is thus that ideals die; not in the conventional pageantry of honoured death, but sorrily, ignobly, while one's head is turned...

- Arnold Bennett, *The Old Wives' Tale*

It is not only the fortunes of men which are equal in America; even their requirements partake in some degree of the same uniformity. I do not believe that there is a country in the world where, in proportion to the population, there are so few uninstructed and at the same time so few learned individuals. Primary instruction is within the reach of everybody; superior instruction is scarcely to be obtained by any. This is not surprising; it is in fact the necessary consequence of what we have advanced above. Almost all the Americans are in easy circumstances, and can therefore obtain the first elements of human knowledge.

- Alexis de Tocqueville, *Democracy in America*, 1835

Introduction

The public school system is a mess. Having taught for two decades in the belly of the beast, I decided seven years ago to write a book about the problems it was enduring and to propose, from what I had learned about its disfunction, what must be done in order to make it work properly. The manuscript to which I dedicated massive amounts of time and reading ended up as eight hundred and thirty-three pages, densely referenced and consisting of thirty four chapters. My original approach was not to make arguments for the problems and their solutions, not as a personal account of teaching tribulations, but to tie objective authority to arguments referencing known experts in the field such as Dewey, Cremin, Ravitch, Bailyn, Adler, Tyack and Cuban and Karier and use their wise insights into current and historic educational policies in making my case. Permissions for referenced material was so fraught with red tape and vagueness that I abandoned this approach fearing bankruptcy by litigious publishers. Any support for this book, drawing on second party referent information, has been removed. The book that I had written would not see print.

This book represents a final attempt at scaling back the objective arguments of the first book to noting the problems as I saw them, subjectively justified, yet containing a proposal for a New School which would address the problems that have kept the public sector from producing a truly democratic school for all American children. The importance of this book is that many of my colleagues and their students who are still in the classroom facing the fallout of academic and disciplinary crippling problems every school day are desperately in need of a functional and worthy learning community. It is certainly for them that this volume is written. This much smaller book identifies the three dilemmas of the public schools: remote leadership, cultural insurgency and run-away student-individualism. The proposed blueprint would address this triple threat as reconstructive organization and operational policies would synchronize to prevent a New School framework from being compromised as the current and past school has been. The New School will allow exemplary academics and a multidirectional learning community. This democratic school would not be a Social School which, for most students, has been the model public institution for education from colonial times. The New School organization would strip academic and communal authority from remote administration and provide legal protection to the school and those that struggle to defend it from the incursion of cultural resistance to uncompromising academics while bringing the recalcitrance of students in line with true educational objectives. The influx of digressive influences which could sideline student education would be immediately given a requirement of scrutinized proof of advantage before being allowed to gain access to the school. A New School disciplinary policy would immediately and diligently guard against threats to learning.

This is not a book about academics, per se, although exemplary academics will only be possible for all when a New School is established and the public school problems are solved by putting realistic solutions to work. Finding answers to problems which are destroying the school are foundational to any attempt to set right the academic course of public education and at long last fulfill a centuries old commitment to the exemplary schooling of America's young.

J. D. Stewart

Chapter 1

The Jumble

Far and few, far and few,
are the lands where the
Jumblies live;
Their heads are green,
and their hands are blue,
And they went to sea in
a sieve.

- Edward Lear,
The Jumblies,

The Jumblies were indeed a jumbled mess; they had green heads and blue hands, conflicted in thought and action, and some of them set to sea in a sieve. They were the fuzzy-headed sailors of Edward Lear's non-sense poem written two hundred years ago. The Jumblies were far from the real world. Jumblies on the shore shouted to the sailors not to set to sea in a sieve because of the stormy and wintery winds, but the sailors did not see themselves as "rash or wrong," and set off anyway. Without a course or itinerary, miraculously the Jumblies' crew returned after wandering aimlessly from shore to shore.

The Jumblies come to mind when I think of American public schools and the pedagogical misadventures that have lead to a failed educational system. Lear's delightful narrative poem captures in metaphor, the problematic tenor of American public education: its jumbled history and modern crisis. The Jumblies on the shoreline cautioned yet reformers never mentioned in their warning that a sieve is not a proper vessel no matter the storm or cold winds. Plans from the educational hierarchy are idealistically green yet academically blue and sadly ineffective in practice. Unwise educational plans and reforms have been rehashed and re-implemented in perpetuity to the inspiration of unendingly unwise thought and action. The Lear poem serves to remind me the endless procession of unwise advice and decisions which have resulted in the misadventure of launching our nation's children into the educational and cultural sea, into the sieve of ill conceived and ill served public education, which has broadly persisted since colonial days. Before we were America, the very system which taught children to read and write in many cases relegated them to classist expectations, limiting some and propelling others to leadership. Piecemeal and shortsighted solutions to educational problems have resulted in an optimistically unwise jumble of thought and action and have sent public education to shores far from democratic, universally academic and culturally responsible policy.

Let it be understood, there is here no intention to degrade the seriousness of the educational practice, the perennial school crisis or the dedication of local administrators and teachers. The educational morass of school practice and management whereby educational mediocrity has been the fare for most public school children demands corrective attention. A triumvirate of influences has prevented public education from serving the exemplary educational needs of all children. Disconnected remote authority, cultural insurgency and extreme individualism are responsible for sinking any hope of a truly democratic education. This *troika* has subjected the school to unwise practice and is holding it for ransom. Cultural drift reckoned by bitter and stormy winds of modernity, jumbling thoughts and practices have driven us repeatedly to distant educational shores. Cultural influence has moved into the school with little attention to its suitability and many young people are commandeering the school for themselves. It is these three influences that must be stopped if public education is ever to be truly exemplary and truly democratic. Painting a rosier picture of the sieve is not nor has it ever been the answer to leaky pedagogy and cultural inappropriateness. American education must be reconstructed.

The American educational system must prepare to launch a seasoned and seaworthy public education policy. I will suggest in these pages the launching of such a school-worthy reconstruction which addresses American public education with realistic optimism which can lift up those in its care, school staff and students, to a high place in academics and social verity.

An alternate methodology will be proposed, not to plug the holes in the unworthy ship, but rather to construct a New school whose successful future requires a loving and immediate intercession of wise practicality, practical but not pragmatic, not whatever works but what works through empathetic reason, openness, hard academics even at risk that the greater culture might not see itself clearly reflected in the process. There should be no requirement that a loose educative understanding from the last two centuries should relegate the learning of the ages to the scrape heap.

The unworkable educational culture and purpose and the progressive disillusionment bred in practicing educators is a good first look at how schools fail teachers and ultimately students. A group of fledgling teachers were interviewed to note their initial impressions of the teaching profession before they entered the classroom. In a follow-up article a few months later after spending time in the classroom, the teachers reported that the actual classroom experience proved other than they were taught to expect. Early on in their teaching assignments these novice teachers found their jobs much more difficult than they ever could have imagined. Placed in poor urban schools, and after only a few months, these idealistic and bright young people were reporting physical exhaustion from an educational process for which they had not been prepared.

Ineffectiveness, a lack of experience and inadequate innate ability were considered possible explanations by the new teachers for what many saw as pending instructional failure. This struggle with self-doubt brought most to redoubled determination. Highly motivated and too proud to admit ultimate failure, some found more time in an otherwise rigorous schedule for generating more interesting lessons. It was hoped that greater student interest would establish meaningful communication and thereby entice students to attentiveness and serious study. Determined to succeed in their new profession, some of the fledglings spent longer hours in preparation of lessons as sleeplessness induced exhaustion became a perennial companion.

The school environment shook the reality of what these teachers thought public education should be. One of the teachers commented that her best friends had a good life, while she virtually had no life at all. Any time off from lesson preparation tended to create at least twinges of ill-preparedness and a modicum of guilt. One teacher temporarily considered teacher insanity to account for the irrational and unreasonable nature of an educational process that left the classroom uncontrollable, teachers in mental anguish and a systematic unreality of praxis.

Self-recrimination and depression were not going to make a bad situation any better. A number of the new teachers considered modifying their teaching methods since teacher education methodologies were proving patently unworkable and virtually unproductive. Teacher expectations and standards were reconsidered; exercises were reconstructed to effect a unanimous mastery of watered-down curricular material. It became clear to at least some of the new teachers that focusing on the "whole student" could be more personally satisfying than attempting to find integrity and professional identity through imparting an uncompromising curriculum to those who were uninterested in learning or who had inadequate preparation for specific subject matter. Such an approach could leave time to enrich those who were actually able to learn and willing to entertain the challenge of learning. But as academic unfruitfulness accompanied loss of basic disciplinary battles, the great thief of instructional time, discipline concerns, were quickly identified by the new teachers as the focus of an unseasoned teacher's day. To develop an escape strategy, one new teacher attempted to put together a reasoned approach to reconstructing the classroom and lessons. Students were still not having fun so the attempt was made to make the lessons even more interesting. Finally some teachers would placate students with lessons that related to their own experience. Hard lessons leave little time for classroom socializing so acting on the preference of the group dynamic, the next step was to loosen the reigns of attempted control and proceed with lessons utilizing interactivity among students rather than teacher directed instruction.

In this way, the classroom, which had not been manageable academically nor always acceptable socially, could address more thoroughgoing cultural needs. By modifying the classroom and instruction, the receptivity of the students to teacher authority and lessons could become more realistically practical. The rationale became clear - teach to the extent that you are able and meet at least minimal standards for student performance. There would, however, be at least two groups to be taught each with different goals and competencies. Leveling to the students' expectations on the one hand and alternatively the academic enrichment of those interested on the other, could be a better, although bifurcated, purpose for instruction rather than that which the new teachers thought they had originally been contracted.

These are some of the tormenting and unproductive concessions made by many fine and energetic young teachers in public schools. In some ways all teachers in the public system experience the nagging of disciplinary and academic compromise. And this is my point: the problem of education in the trenches is the loss of authority to administer and teach the precious children in public school care. No teacher can correct it by better methods or more creative lessons. The problem is systemic. Given this story is not an isolated instance of educational insipidity, the question of what can be done over the whole of public education in America to bring excellence to the school room must arise. Indeed, specific underlying problems need to be addressed in consideration of reconstruction of the public school whose educational practice has been culturally compromised and politically corrupted.

No doubt a number of those new teachers in my story will remain among the ranks of teachers who have maintained their stations, fought through the novice years and survived to teach to the extent to which they are permitted. These young teachers have found themselves among the ranks of veterans who have seen the signs of defeat - lack of student seriousness and the undisciplined and pedestrian nature of student-individuals within the school culture. Yet seasoned teachers remain in the profession to accomplish what they can with the students they are allowed to teach.

Educational excellence in public school classrooms, despite the efforts of well meaning and hard working teachers and local administrators, is not working for all students even when many of the more debilitating problems of which many schools face are not present. In some ways the symptoms of school problems have always been the same and have never been solved as students, or at least some students, have always been indisposed to school authority and educational rigor. But today we face a stronger and more confident rebellion made critical by a growing minority of discontented and distracted student-individuals. We are witnessing a cultural tsunami that is raised against fairness and reason. While the school's authority has been forfeited by the cultural attendants, the reforming experts on the shore, who see no problem in schools which tread dangerous cultural currents, public education, for all practical purposes, has gone under weakened by the influences of a raging stormy cultural sea.

We have tried program after program to repair the public school system. Although most citizens have an opinion about public education in America and many of those would admit that the system, as it is, is ill conceived and practiced, yet fewer would acknowledge, for the very reasons that have created a diverse understanding of what education has come to represent, that there are major educational problems that are not teacher, local administrator or curriculum related. For those who have a vested interest in massaging education for reasons other than those educational and academic, there will be no admission that there is indeed a failed public educational system. Some because of staid philosophic dedication, others for unfailing optimism, while others for self-interest, all bare the responsibility for the continued support for failing schools.

Dancing around the practical issues of the classroom must come to an end. Teachers and local administrators deal with what amounts to voluntary servitude and perpetual anger over the procedural hocus-pocus which often overshadows this most amazing occupation. On reflection and in studying the history of public education from early colonial times, the black magic of bureaucratic pedagogy began to be revealed as a cumulative historical and unending cultural assaults on the public school, its operatives and its students. A most glaring realization that often stirred me from my sleep was the realization that solving the problems of education by addressing foundational problems of the school would not be possible unless attention to individual school needs and consequent policies were preeminent in the repair process. Schools, staff and students do not need more or new reforms especially those offered by remote management, the boards and departments of education, but reconstruction.

Organizational practices need to be practical, local and immediately responsive to the academic and social needs of teachers, students and administrators. Reforms, however, always come from outside the practice of the classroom and generally consists of what the culture thinks that education needs but what is in reality a social   educational program foisted on the school because it is easily manipulated from outside. The solutions imposed are not usually appropriate to correcting the problem of a school but are blanket edicts handed down for all schools whether needed or not. The jumbles and conflicts in public education arise from inappropriate policy decisions or oversight which often leave principals, staff and students to either make the system work locally or at least make it appear to work. It is left to the individual schools to correct policy where there is educational malpractice on the part of remote administration without bringing too much attention to the local school's attempt at a self fix. Each school is left to rightly recognize and take responsible action in defending the school against disruptive agency.

For teachers, weighed down each year by their ever mounting bureaucratic burdens, relief cannot come too quickly. Most teachers and administrators want a quick fix because they are immersed in suffocating minutia of day-to-day school operations while being expected to also teach and manage its politically correct baggage. No one can deal with an issue of academics without first addressing discipline concerns and not this without consulting the Delphian oracles elected and unelected to divine self-protective panaceas. The teacher subsequently feels the mind-boggling stupor of resignation in compromise with the acceptance of the inevitable and more profound sense of personal as well as professional betrayal. That is the way the system works or rather the way that schools do not work well. This must be changed.

Having no real authority, teachers must focus on contriving a workable loyalty to minister to the mood of the policy touters. The educational theorists and seers view real school problems impassively from the jumbled shoreline, onlookers optimistically viewing the potentially disastrous educational prospects of teacher and students, while schools struggle to deal with real issues and real problems. The federal, state and local educational authorities look through their dark lenses knowing what they want to see for the school system, which is seldom educational and at each level, as it is passed down, too remote to really know the full impact of any decisions. Policy changes are handed down as the real world tangentially threatens the political-safety and remoteness of those on the shore. Officials of public education hate to hear their phones ring for fear of litigation. Having school policy challenged in print or being pressured from seats of higher political power does not necessarily impact the classroom but sends the Illuminati scrambling for protection from the fallout of being out of touch, ill-informed or uninformed.

Although remote administrators seem to be very reasonable, nice people, yet only on special occasions do teachers find opportunities to talk to a board member in the school. Their appearances generally signal some inestimable emergency, and they materialize to put out any fires, divert blame or take a defensive posture in spinning a politically correct New Speak. How do these phantom rulers know about the acceptability of their teachers? Are teachers academically sound? Are they good people with disciplinary strategies that reliably defuse difficult situations in the classroom? Remote evaluation admits to acceptability on the basis of a teacher's name not coming up in a board meeting or before a remote administrator in connection with some public relations nightmare which could possibly reflect on administration and the school system.

What can a remote administrator know of the classroom the students and curriculum from a position outside of the school. Being politically savvy does not solve problems in public education, and without superior information about the classroom and a willingness to support schools even at personal and political loss, there can be little to no meaningful leadership and appropriate directives. Teachers and local administration sacrifice self every day in the classroom for the art and science of teaching and for the betterment of their students. They lead by doing and often under the unreasonable expectations of the system which is physically broken. School staff must then devise workable policy for those ineffective directives forthcoming from the policy makers. Without effective leadership and informed decision making, the teacher is left to litigious parents or parental surrogate accusers without the benefit of aid from remote superiors.

And the cultural wars rage on. Teachers are often left to the media and the lawyers lest a public relations fallout could prove damaging to the school system's image; in which case matters may be hushed up, money may be offered to salve the victim in lieu of court settlements and publicity, and the teachers fired or reassigned. In this the teacher stands alone while public education either rightly or wrongly, yet historically, takes on a losing defensive posture and surrenders, court case by court case, the power to educate and civilize the young. In the midst of an unstable classroom, turmoil, challenges to authority, and even under the threat of litigations, the teacher tries to teach. The teacher hopes to have taught some, those usually with the encouragement of parents and stable homes, those who have pushed to learn despite the disruptive nature of the few who for lack of restraint, embolden by selfishness and hubris, become the disciplinarily unteachable. Teachers cannot teach, if parents do not allow them, if parents put their children's winning above student education.

Today's public school teacher must face the prospects of conditions which threaten academic excellence. Striving to cause no irreversible damage to those that cannot be taught or those who are prevented from receiving less instructive attention, teaching is nonetheless sidetracked by time-consuming non-academic issues. Like crippling paperwork, teaching becomes less about instruction than meeting educational system goals which stand for the defense of the system. Disregard any sense that culpability is only to be found in the remote directors of education, this is a false impression. Those within the school who are given the responsibility to carry out school purpose bear some weight of responsibility, if not the bulk of the emotional scars. Though there is little hope of finding real and lasting solutions to the problems of public education as sought after by politicians and remote educational bureaucrats, school failure is invariably laid at the feet of all the hard working school staff, who have no authority to address systemic problems.

Local administrators are in fear or have serious concerns that a parent or lawyer will successfully challenge the working procedures of the school. The principals, often out of defensive action, may massage the rules according to the sensed fears of their superiors and take direct hits in disagreements with the public. When a rule is needed to allow the school to run smoothly and safely and is challenged successfully, then it makes tenuous any further use of the rule, a dangerous precedent, since a successful high profile challenge of rules may render rules of little authority by the courts, the public system across America could suffer.

One lost battle can affect a whole school system and even other school systems through court rulings. Compromise is the result of fear of lost options as pernicious issues flood campuses adding to the ineffective management of discipline problems and becoming an omen of further threats to an ever waning school authority. School principals stand in the gate to defend the school with increasingly more ineffective weapons to forestall challenges to authority. One wrong decision and the principal may exact the cold scrutiny of his superiors spurred on by the immediate culture of parents and students demanding repentance or even replacement of the school staff members. Local school administration is a job for dedicated heroes who are willing to rock the boat to maintain personal and school integrity, stand for exemplary education and hope that their efforts will give teachers another day in which teaching students might be the main thrust of a united school staff effort. Lost of authority prevents a dedicated singularity of academics.

The student body is constituted of students and student-individuals. Student-individuals are in attendance primarily not to learn but to perform and strut while attempting to meet the minimal legal requirements of compulsory education. Dedicated students, on the other hand, are given to learning, while enduring the selfish and patently unlawful disruption by student-individuals who view learning as at least a secondary consideration of their education. Rebellion is often abetted by parents who either overtly subvert the work of educating their children or ignore the child's social, behavioral and academic needs. Students, dedicated students, despite the disruptive student-individual influence, work at getting an education hoping for a successful future and depending on study to realize opportunity. In contrast, student-individuals pose, socialize, protest regulations, and by their actions demand recognition of the myth that it is their school. They plaintively, physically endure classes and hold education in low regard. Mentally and financially they are often over-invested in part-time employment while saving for the purchase of a newer automobile or some newer innovative widget.

The broader culture supports and directs these children's affectations. Finding acceptance in the student-individualist culture requires uniform thought and usually superficial evidence as proof of allegiance such as the style of dress. While the student, by contrast, works to develop an inner life for an unknown future, the student-individual adopts a exterior identity that brings with it a culturally approved set of generally unanalyzed dogmas in loose montage tacitly prescribed by the authority of a ghostly cadre of idealists. Student-individualists are superficially linked through a pseudo-culture of identity which is in reality in rebellion against all authority except the individual authority of the One, for which their numbers stand. Student-individualism membership is identifiable as simulation or even simulacrum of a manufactured group image. For to belong in support of a common unflinching purpose is not the goal of the group, since the group is perpetually shape-shifting, changing ideological talking points and evolving new dress-images.

School is not important to the student-individual, but almost everything else is: everything for which borrowed identity depends: the look, the identifiers of membership. Apart from the fact that student-individuals are not of their own making, either due to adverse personal history or merely the need to belong, they tend to be disruptive and degrade the process of education for themselves and others, the dedicated students and the rest of the school community. Going through the motions to get by, they contribute nothing to the school community while taking away the opportunity for others to get an education. This is an aggressive insistence on indiscriminate cultural absorption for *pro forma* self-identity, a disguise, that compromises the student's true experiential development. The ephemeral student-individual is capable of destroying lessons, even classrooms and ultimately schools, since in their disguise he or she will act out but not attend to lessons or let others do so. These students need to be saved from their own formulaic and fabricated failures. For those that remain, the students, the future will hold to one of two divergent paths. From the beginning of public education and before, the young were fitted to their work by either being trained to a minimal level of literacy or given a broader education for future leadership. This dual path has plagued our country from colonial days. For most of the youth citizenry, for other than potential leaders, there will only be a minimal education.

As with the Jumblies, education's problems stem from a unrelenting prescriptive culture. It does not matter that the history of public education has been the result of many great names with high ideals, with practical goals for children; education has all gone wrong while it was being attended to, "sorrily, ignobly" as heads were "turned" from broadly educational purpose. For truly we all are disadvantaged by an inequitable and inferior public education system. The student, however, is directly at risk and cannot afford the loss of an optimistic future and the rigor of educational excellence. In order for students to win, schools must win the right to educational authority with which it struggles. Our failure to begin reconstruction, rethinking of American public education, will once again result in failure for both students, student-individuals, school cultures and academics. Proper reconstruction will result in the public school's victory and will be a victory for all Americans.

Chapter 2
Legacy

Many a reformer perishes in his removal of rubbish; and that makes the offensiveness of the class. They are partial; they are not equal to the work they pretend. They lose their way in the assault on the kingdom of darkness they expend all their energy on some accidental evil, and lose their sanity and power of benefit.

- Ralph Waldo Emerson, Essays

It will never be known what acts of cowardice have been motivated by the fear of not looking sufficiently progressive.

- Charles Peguy, *Notre Patrie*

Education as a public institution arose from a colonial and early American desire to have a functionally educated citizenry. Many young people, that were part of family or community businesses and needed to be able to read and write to the extent of their duties as business employees, were minimally equipped as literate functionaries. When public education was finally instituted it consisted usually of only a few years while those that were bred for leadership received a far more exalted education. While most were meant for labor, the elite were sent to higher education. Many young Americans were educated in private schools which were supported by religious denominations. It was from private education, where education began centuries before and a continent away, that many of the future leaders of the colonies and early America were to matriculate.

In early America, the industrial revolution gave business and industry a stake in the use of public education for obtaining a labor force. Eventually occupational training would find its way into the curriculum and those not inclined to academics, or those not born to greatness, would most probably find much of their education in pursuit of a life of labor. Government leaders wanted the citizenry to have at least minimal literacy in order that they could better select their leaders from an elite stable of thoroughbreds, grown for the purpose of governance and serving in highly educated professions. Women and minorities were to eventually receive educational opportunities, but the educationally chosen, the future leaders, would receive considerably more educative attention and would be given a broader curriculum for success.

The progressive era of education which started late in the nineteenth century and continued into the first decades of the twentieth century, although it has never been officially interred, came in many of its variant forms to prescribe a bifurcated path for students in public education. With the appearance of superintendents and other educational bureaucrats, education was to begin to look more like a business than a school. Education was tied to budgets and thus controlled by non-educators. Decisions that were to direct educational institutions for the next century were to be arrived at following a business appropriation model overseen by a superintendent and his or her foot soldiers. The exacerbation of educative purpose by the remote school authorities would be seen, eventually and without much dissension, as the accepted approach to school management. In the name of public education, the bureaucracy was very often making inappropriate decisions based on budget and social concerns, academics ultimately were to be routinely compromised by this remote control. What could be taught, who would be taught and what was conceded to the remote school leadership, these compromised the spirit of academics.

If one does not, cannot or will not understand education and forward its purpose, then socialization by cultural standards is the most likely default, and the American public system has suffered under this mediocre bureaucratic standard. An educational reform movement that produced another compromise to public education was advanced by the progressive educational movement which held the belief that bureaucrats, many of them either unfamiliar with teaching and its methodologies or those that were not particularly interested in committing to a career in the classroom, could make flawless even metric decisions about student abilities and set each appropriately on the proper path to a life of labor or leadership. This is still an unquestioned function of bureaucrats in the public system. The tragedy is that this decision once made and implemented will more often result in the students trained to labor never being able to extricate themselves to pursue hopes of greater expectations, since time either eats up the educational opportunities for greater success or the tracking of students to lower level coursework will more than likely divert any serious considerations of more academic plans.

For some the progressive era saw the student become the bearer of an unerring divine spark. This romantic take on the innocence of the child was to result in the abdication of adult authority leaving the school unable or unwilling to control wanton anti-educational and uncivil youth. Among the waning authority of remote leadership and the unswerving incursion of cultural mandates, many modern youth have been permitted to enter into a life of extreme student-individualism unchecked by school policy. It is remote leadership, and insurgent culture with which this third disruption to the public education system has combined to bring destructive influences which hold the modern school hostage, deny its academic calling and prevent exemplary education for all.

The failure of the school is not seen in clear focus. The remote boards and authorities make decisions that are political and not educational. Decisions by higher-school leadership tend to be more about political advancement or the aspiration to move up to more prestigious, non-educational government positions. Orchestrated by the mavens of metrics, in the name of service to the system, the remote dignitaries, have, in their attempt to modernize the school, found little efficiency and often very little educational commitment. If this seems a hard accusation, then consider my experience and other classroom teachers who have rarely seen board members attend classes to see the effect that their decisions or lack of decision making have had on the course of local education. Still the layers of bureaucracy continued to be added one on top of another until governmental oversight of the schools, for academics and school communities, has resulted in a sort of indentured servitude for many students whose life work may be fixed in a secondarily rigorous course of study. This is ironically reminiscent of colonial businesses which often used the family young as laborers seemingly in a caring and protective outpouring of familial love, while actually according little hope of advancing young worker fortunes or occupational opportunities.

Minimal education rarely promotes success yet when it occurs it is much publicized. Most successful people have put education squarely in the middle of their plans, but, when success is realized in its rare occurrence outside of an educationally directed plan, the isolated example seems to become the rule rather than an exception. Steve Jobs and Bill Gates are always mentioned when school is seen as unnecessary. These were exceptionally bright people who had been accepted to an ivy league university system and who fell into an historic innovational application whose time was right. Both never tapped into the greatest discovery of all: the perpetuation of the academically educated mind. Entertainment showcases successful and wealthy performers whose dreams came true without the necessity of a bonafide education. This becomes the pipe dream for many, that they may avoid college and beyond and their success will justify not pursuing advanced degrees. Both of these examples are unrealistic and let students off the hook for pursuit of an education-based career and provides an escape for those not wanting to commit to study and hard work. Professional athletes send the message that you can forego school and still make millions playing a game for a living. Thus the young are given the out to dwell on success by fiat, and when rarely attained, it further perpetuates false hope in the easily led and lazy who will almost surely find only a life of labor when they wake. The schools have contributed to this somnambulism which allows students to complete a low-level degree, pass objective end of year tests and walk across a stage to reduced intellectual options for the future.

The failure that most see as a glaring need for reform in public education is the low level of student-learning competency, but this cannot be addressed until the school is reconstructed to account for these three foundational failures which conspire against the education of American school-age children. All attempts to improve public education while allowing these detrimental effects to linger have failed broadly and will continue to fail. A score of new educational and feel-good extracurricular programs will never bring school success. Most students know this. A failed academic paradigm, a scam consisting of dubious fact without comprehensive context and deep discussion, will never convince students that education is anymore than a hazing contest that it is not what you know and how you know it but how well you play the game. The problem is not made better by the theoretical learning programs which try to make learning fun and have never been seriously questioned or adequately vetted. These are refitted, renamed and re-spun assuming all the ideologically failed ideas about children, what education is and the sacrosanct process of letting the children guide their own efforts to learning. The charlatans who promote this drivel and never analyze the appropriateness of any program to the school or its students - one size fits all - retool with programs that never violate their misinformed ideology. Yet none of the programs are really seen to fail because they are perfectly coherent within the ideological understanding that spawned them. This is the only result of an ongoing process of public school reform, business as usual. Reconstruction of a New School would commence without assumptions and chart a course that would allow a reflective and advanced methodology of rhetoric, discipline and civility.

We must end the pedagogical fakery begun in the past centuries in America. Schools must be given the authority to address the symptoms of each school's needs both socially and academically to establish reasonable criteria for establishing authority for protecting all students, in consideration of each school, and insure that all students get an education and not just those that are intellectually superior or motivated to learn. Schools need to stand up against the courts and the culture, to the student-individualism that destroys school community and reestablish standards that cannot be controverted to the exclusive draw of business, the self-serving of politicos, ideologues, idealists and theoreticians on the jumbled shore. The schools must escape the numbing touch of the remote administrations of education, those of government and the collegiate education departments. The remote boards of education who orchestrate the failure in bureaucratic lock-step must be denied authority to treat each school as if each school demographic was the same.

The teaching staff of public schools spends time, wasted by bureaucrats, filling out paperwork instead of spending valuable time on lesson preparation and using the remainder to ward off exhaustion. Teachers and local administration try to maintain professionalism as remote authority saps the creative and authoritative effectiveness of the classroom which has been historically sacrificed to a business model of efficiency, metric valuation and temporality; these continue to jumble any broad efforts to remove deleterious societal influences which have placed ruinous restrictions on the public school. Reconstruction must meet these intrusions with preemptive defensive actions which will be labeled coercive action by many. This approach is the only way to guarantee that student can learn as they should and disruptive students are given a chance to learn rather than ultimately being shown the back door of the school house.

Chapter 3
Principles of Reconstruction:
The Authentic Sign

We desire to be made great; we desire to be
touched with that fire which shall command
this ice to stream, and make our existence a
benefit... The reason why any one refuses
his assent to your opinion, or his aid to your
benevolent design, is in you: he refuses to
accept you as a bringer of truth, because
though you think you have it, he feels that
you have it not. You have not given him the
authentic sign.

-Ralph Waldo Emerson, Essays

The authentic sign of exemplary public education will be found in the provision of education for all with all opportunities assumed. What stands between the school and achieving this goal is that the context of our educational problem today is inseparable from that of the larger cultural crisis. With a modicum of reason and common sense, theories of pedagogy are thrown at school problems as if those problems are resolvable within and alone by exclusively removing them and yet failing to see the larger context. Theory, without hope of confirming experiential evidence, ideology, is not dependable for launching meaningful school improvement. The methodological error is that real solutions can only be arrived at from fruitful practice. The culture has made inroads into the school and as a result has become education. Not only is the cultural contribution not academic it has supplanted learning in its name. Cultural substitution cannot solve school problems. Historical success can be measured by recalling that polio was wiped out by vaccination, a positive health problem eradicated, using the school as an organizational tool to award immunity to a population in jeopardy. On the other hand, racial integration was a bandaid approach with less obvious positive benefits for establishing a country of pluralism and tolerance. The schools became the medium for equality as whites moved to the suburbs and minority schools remained, and both became even more intrenched in their distinct tribal identities. Elitist schools and often dangerous dumbed down schools were the result of this social tinkering. Now looking at a failed attempt at using schools to do the hard work of socialization, even in an honest moment of reflection by progressives, could only result in the admission that our socialized children have fallen behind in educational ranking among other industrial nations and the learning community has been compromised by the extra-educational culture. All influences allowed into the school enter on supposition and speculation, just as the plan to uniformly socialize America, and, like this fiasco, many have been found unworkable. Social education is oxymoronic. Social issues need to be seriously addressed, but feeding students or protecting them from abusive situations should be effectively handled outside the school because the balance of total-child needs has, in effect, been responsible for tipping the public school away from the academic education that all children need.

The social school is not an authentic sign of an exemplary educational school. Authority must be attained by clear and actionable policy not caving to every social problem. Any distractions from the academic school environment, those influences which could interfere with this mandate to attend and deliver education to all, must be removed. Cultural imperatives which become distractions, which produce division in the school program, must be eliminated. Can an American public school system be reconstructed with the goal of focusing exclusively on the education of all students without the influx of cultural correctness or external pressures? Can the school stand against the drone of society, oppose syncretic dissolution of the school and, against protest, require student and student-individualist to enter into the richness of challenging and reasoned course work? These are most pressing questions; the immediate answer is truthfully, no. Unless basic academic and social requirements are met, specifically designed to avoid such non-intellectual interference, there can be no assurance that such changes are possible. Unless by the empowering of local educators to recast the school in a form for which hard work can be a reward for the teachers and offer educational promise for all students change is impossible.

In order to redirect education for the interest of all students, a New School must be constructed. An aggressive version of reconstruction would provide an immediate turnaround of schools while garnering claims of coercion from the self-righteous ranks of rancor, the educationally remote. A light version of reconstruction could be a more immediately doable framework, more realistic in that the remote administration is spared the reductionist axe where a slower more peaceful self-rule is chosen. Both approaches are not to be mistaken for reforms. The re-making of school by either approach is a foundational change. Reformation failure as an approach to solving school problems cannot be considered viable; such attempts have done nothing improving in the past and portend nothing more useful in the future for radically improving public education. Only by reconstruction can a New and worthy school be given to the public.

Malpractice has produced an indeterminate authority within the school. Each school's needs, policies and regulations, must be developed by teachers and local administrators on site. Blind direction by remote boards who have little familiarity with specific school issues hand down rulings ostensibly based on the needs that are considered for all schools in the district. Their direction is usually a compromise of local authority, negotiated with students, parents and lawyers. Identifying and establishing what will be referred to here as redoubts, the New School defenses depose obstacles to teaching allowing school community self-rule to be put in place quickly and appropriately in response to school-spoiling problems without the dependence on one-size-fits-all proceduralism. On the battlefield redoubts are movable defenses that usually can be erected or taken down quickly as needed. Redoubts may be used to address obstacles to learning, discipline and cultural intrusion in individual schools according to real needs and before those needs become insurmountable or even become inculcated in common educational practice. A radical reconstruction for developing an academic and social climate in which American children can be successfully taught requires a ground-up not a top-down approach.

At the heart of the issue is what public education is and how it should be advanced and reclaimed as a valued public institution. Education must be seen as possessing hardline academic programs that will prepare any student-graduate of the public system to pursue any career, and experience the depth of learning necessary to establish a personal stronghold of knowledge in the world and to stoke an unquenchable fire for learning through reason and language such that a lifelong education will ensue. Expectations less than this should be unacceptable and are unjustifiable. It is on the pillars of pedagogy that a New School must arise, reconstructed and protected from erosive influences.

There will be a small number of students who will need extensive and meticulous learning care, but, when students are evaluated as either superior, average or limited in capacity, assumptions with life-long consequences are set in motion. In reality it is often the pedagogical evaluators that are limited; they are limited in scope by reductionist proceduralism, and a lesser education is often divined by predilection of methodology which though favored may only be authoritatively substantiated by grasping at theoretical straws. The remote bureaucracy as an oversight group directing public education must be replaced. Their viable aid in school policy must be viewed as extremely doubtful by the most sanguine optimist seeking proof of exemplary education for all public school students. Where educational construction, local school capital improvement, procuring of materials in bulk for all district schools at better prices, and, where collective undertaking can be better managed, a central authority could be a valuable aid to the schools. Purchasing texts and maintaining the schools physical plants could prove a useful function for boards of education. However, decision-making power concerning educational curriculum and micromanagement must be wrested from politics, if American schools are to become the model for academics worldwide. Remote and political influence determining educational policy is destructive to the public school, to teachers, local administration and students who depend on the school community to help make high-level decisions concerning their academic education.

Assuming that the school could be reconstructed with academics at the core of the educational process, there would be several requirements, or an authentic sign of excellence. First, the teachers would have to be given the protected right to teach without the interjection of non-instructional requirements placed ahead of academics. Sports, jobs, cars, family vacations should not trump the legal requirement for children to attend school. Legislation that is now on the books concerning attendance must be enforced. Students must attend school, if not otherwise approved for home study or private education. And in this respect, boards if allowed to remain in any capacity as a true support for schools, should logically become the perfect lobbyists against cultural and social interference with and within the school. If a board were to survive in a New School environment, then it must be considered non-political and strictly without supervisory authority. Seemingly the only way to rid the school of remote intervention, if reconstruction could not be managed, is for schools to secede from school districts after gaining voter support to fund their independence and to actively pursue judicial challenges to state and national compliance regulations, agreeing to do what is practically possible for all students and seeking court approval to disregard the remaining over-reach of remote governance. If board and oversight authorities would help education they would serve everyone by getting out of the business of school academics and socialization. Individual schools could maintain autonomy and teach yet, still for mutual benefit, band together to meet legal challenges. There could be great advantage in contracting together to truthfully represent the educational necessity of academic education for all students and stand as one against the long arm of state and federal intrusions.

Second, the schools would have to develop and consistently deal with academics and discipline with a real and effective no-tolerance enforcement policy. This could only be done under direct control of the law enforcement authorities backed up by a legal staff employed expressly to facilitate an uninterrupted education for the children in the care of the school and for dedicated teachers and school staff to carry out their compulsory roles within legal guidelines as pedagogical experts. Boards could take on the fight of legal challenges against each schools attempt to provide exemplary education as one of its newly constructed assignments.

What if each school were allowed to make local decisions about education and the running of each school. This idea has produced charter schools which are allowed to instigate their own rules of pedagogy and student retention. Unfortunately with mixed academic results, some of these schools have proved to be no more academic than the schools they may have replaced. Allowing school to do what they need to do for themselves could be as much a formula for failure, if ill-conceived and misdirected, as is allowing boards to control in isolation and from a distance the fate of each school. Academics must be put first in any reconstruction with the education of all students being the ultimate local school goal.

Third, there should be a clear separation of instructional and administrative staff decisions. Indeed, all educational decisions must be made without political intervention. This will with all effort insure that teachers will be given the right to pursue an uninterrupted, challenging curriculum. Inquiry based on course information should be the recurrent format for all classes with grades given for participation and intellectual interaction among students. The modern culture is not capable of keeping its bias out of education and therefore must necessarily be among the topics that intelligent discussion pursues. Students must objectively understand the role that the culture would play in their lives. There is no reason that an open and critical discussion of the culture should be out of bounds for students, who, once graduated, must face the culture alone and on its own terms. School may be the only place in which the right to openly question societies assumptions about adult life may be fairly and rationally approached without taking the absorbed understanding from the drone of the media and its mavens. Educated students must be able to critique cultural influences on their lives. For those in charge, servicing the immediate needs of students has been raised to fanatical status among the modern theorists and theory-rights merchants. Pivotable to any determination to reconstruct education there must be protection from unexamined and destructive incursions by the culture of prestige into the academic workings of the public school. If there were to be a critical inquiry, it would better be the students looking objectively at their education and the world that awaits outside the school house door, ready to give the only understanding of a world which they must navigate. Therefore, teaching deeply, in rhetoric and the classics, presupposes exemplary students who could discuss cultural problems and inquire into solutions to those problems. Objectivity in education can thus be arrived at and may be derived from the severing of schools from social programs allowing students to wrestle with those issue in an open classroom critique. Social programs should be handled away from and outside of the schools and school hours which would prevent the curricular indoctrination of political and educational correctness.

Fourth, reconstruction must provide for divorcing education from politics, government, theory mills and business. This is a corollary of calling for an unbiased and open discussion of the critical culture which often education currently gives blanket acceptance. The academic policy makers must be academic themselves. In business there would be strong reluctance to hand over the reigns of corporate America to the artists or the poets and with good reason. Life and death issues hinging on surgery should not be left in the hands of an expert in foreign affairs. Nor would we feel that the country was well off in the hands of a political leader whose only claim to fame was winning the lottery. Elections may have more to do with fashionable ideology more than the ability of candidates to make wise changes in the way that government and schools are managed. So why do we allow those to take charge of academic school decision-making and school operations who have no immediate first-hand knowledge of schools and who may not even be concerned about schools or try to learn about what really happens in the halls and classrooms and who do little to nothing to offset their ignorance?

Fifth, each school does need to interface with non-educational professions to aid in its task, those expert in budgets, legal issues and law enforcement should be integral to new school reconstruction, They need to bring their talents to the aid of the school which must keep the politicos at a distance, while these professionals in their fields are allowed to help each school provide for the raising of the educational bar through real contributions to the academic focus of the school.

Sixth, the certification of teachers must not be a doctrinaire bottleneck to classroom uniformity, a monopolizing influence in the teaching profession. No teacher should be expected to become one of the pedagogical cadre by dancing through hazing hoops. This does not guarantee that teachers understand what teaching is and what desirable outcomes of student education must be. Remote leadership should have no directive authority in the school for its goals are not primarily educational and if educational inroads are attempted by boards and district heads they merely echo the complicitous mantra with that of the education mills that turns out what will ultimately result in disillusioned and defeated teachers serving up formulaic pap for students. Teachers must be encouraged to develop a technical and philosophical pedagogy and develop a defense and strategy for teaching not just the curriculum but beyond the curriculum addressing those issues of learning that transcend any particular course of study. Furthermore, the teacher needs to be a model of citizenship for students answerable to the local administration and students but not controlled by the latter. For the form of educational practices goes far beyond the direct substance of the lesson to example and application. Calling attention to the real significance of a lesson in example and application while deflecting from one's on life practice is hypocrisy. The true mark of education, so distinctly apart from training, is that it must be given the weight of embodied metaphysical reason and ethically actionable behavior, as modeled authority. Training cannot be taken as personal behavioral objectification. There is a difference in application for application sake in training a student to occupational labor and using understanding to direct inquiry into metaphysical insightfulness. It is easier to provide a talking head for lessons, but only people can labor to produce a learning community, a school, which does not evade the wolves at the door but rakes through the greater society and the community outside the school to learn and reason with others to meet the ultimate test of learning - its use in life in reasonable thought and action.

Seventh, the Romantic views of the child and student must be fervently denied since this is an appeal to the authority of the young who are ignorant of the broader world, their present and their potential. A child, a student, can be taught without having to concede to them a romantic nature or even divinity. Any teacher concerned for the academic advancement of each child and having spent time in the classroom has had cause to doubt anything close to adolescent divinity and so, from experience, has had more than adequate proof for blanket denial. The Romantic idea of the child in *Emile* did not prevent Rousseau from maintaining his authority when the fictional Emile brought control issues into dispute. The lesson is that children cannot be left to their own devices to become educated and find their own way.

Eighth, the practice of educational tracking or paths must be eliminated for it is another failed way to view children in educational pursuits. For those that are not dedicated to learning, school counseling does a disservice to those relatively unmotivated students by denying the developmental capacity of each student and the potential for future growth of interests and expectations. In essence the bureaucrats are making decisions based on disputable theories concerning each student's future, not far from reading tea leaves or measuring the phrenological bumps on students' heads. When an assessment of a child's immediate abilities is determined and from that assessment assumptions are made about the potential for further intellectual development, resultant tracking puts the child on a path that is most likely to accord a self-fulfilling prophesy. When students are repeatedly channeled to lesser stimulating classwork and may opt to take training in some lesser course work, their future is most often predetermined. School staff advisors should not be allowed to overreach in the life-changing decisions about the curriculum for each student.

Ninth, reconstruction principles must acknowledge that public education is composed of schools which are realistically faithful to the practice of true pluralistic communities. The manipulative derailing of cultural pluralism was seen in the integration of schools in the fifties and sixties. Historically, failure to integrate the hearts and minds of communities in dedication to equality was laid on the public schools as education interceded in the social ill of racial discrimination. The loss of community schools to threatening cultural differences that had no referent neighborhood connections was to drive families to the suburbs and private schools, disrupt the academic atmosphere of schools left behind, and create institutional discrimination among schools some of which were selectively advantaged to retain students in exclusivity or in specialty schools. It must have seemed a wise move on the part of the business community to put the burden of long overdue equality of education on the back of the school. Although more politically and certainly economically unacceptable, seeing that housing represents one of the prime indicators of the economic pulse of business and personal ownership, subsidizing the integration of neighborhoods, nevertheless, would in the long run have gone a long way to remove many social inequities that were exacerbated by the political influences in the one-time neighborhood schools.

But the economy was given preference to the equal education and socialization of all students. True integration could have in time found social acceptance among a truer pluralistic community and as a foundational change in defining a true policy of social pluralism. Yet, the legislators and theorists would protect the financial interests of the housing market and continue a phase of segregation from which we have not been extricated. The richest have not condescended to the public schools following so called integration of public education no matter the quality of education, but finding public education set aside in racially protected enclaves, moved their children to private schools or home schooled them.Those groups left behind in the city usually went to schools mostly comprised of students from their own culture, and depending on the demands placed on those schools, students could not always find a wide range of worthy academic programs from school to school that were on par with those enjoyed in the private sector or the suburbs. Families moved to avoid unwanted school culture and those unable to move took what schools they were given. Integration and equality came to mean the same thing, yet the policy, for all practical purposes, was still "separate but equal." The preservation of the housing market in the short run resulted in a segregated educational system, one not necessarily based on homogeneous racial make up but generally similar socioeconomic status within the student body.

Plurality in the twentieth century was not the result, and there was loss of toleration and often hatred across school districts. The animosity and cultural disparity among races and those ultimately headed for labor without clear choice in the matter has created a condition that could hardly be described as socially pluralistic. Despite heroic efforts to bring the races together the results have been less than encouraging. Cultures and races separated during the second half of the twentieth century have given rise to unalloyed expectations which have raised, it would appear, an impenetrable wall among many racial spokesmen and political pundits. The fear that big money and power, a legacy from colonial and early American times, would continue to disrupt the process of integrating the people of our country is still being realized. Recent attempts to reorder neighborhoods through pluralistic redistribution has resulted in failure of intended inter-social engineering. Educational equality outside of an academic school will only arrive with socioeconomic equality. This is, in point of fact, a case of the cart before the horse.

Tenth, schools must deal with pluralistic issues that stand between people by bringing to bare rules of disciplinary engagement without favoritism and grounded in the rule for the many regardless of race, ethnicity or religion. Cultural representatives need to reduce the divisive rhetoric in order that all can have a real shot at the American dream and not be insulated from finding success in the culture by absorbing the dogma and bias of leaders with ulterior motives of self-importance.

An eleventh principle of reconstruction turns on the real purpose of public education. Should the purpose of a newly reconstructed school be to equip graduates to gain more wealth or to gain power over others? Or should education not be considered first for personal betterment but to gain an understanding of the world and how to improve it for all, to consider the needs of others, which requires the developing of an understanding of others, and to coalesce by consensus on issues to which all can agree and to gain a genuine insight into the rational and irrational reasons for an inability to form a consensus on issues? The pure measure of pedagogy is to develop agile minds balanced with reason, good judgment, empathy and compassion. Short-sightedness, looking for immediate drastic progress in education will prove hopelessly unproductive and portends failure. Dogma, power and prejudice must be rooted out and this only by long and arduous attention to the good of all members of the school community and through true communication among all members. To know others, to care about others, to give our lives in the service of others as well as ourselves, is the message. Not to resound our own goodness, we must live lives of service in action. To see Others as ourselves, in the form of a true educational community, not separate, not secondarily considered, but inseparable from all, having the ability to be the best we can be will allow admirable models of self-sacrificing heroes, role models, to rise in admiration for this is the challenge to us all, to our view of our responsibility to those of the school community and beyond.

The twelfth principle concerns academics, without which the school can be no better than a social club. Any new school reconstruction must face the challenge of a difficult and comprehensive curriculum offered to all students. The hard work of learning in the classroom is good practice in unification of self with others. Education cannot be in a larger sense learning for self in hopes that others will fail in their pursuits and become unaccomplished victims and we the victors. Neither can school be sanctioned as essentially a proofer of brain function with the reward for a quick mind being special grooming for success.

Academics is crushed under the weight of social programs that in effect de-emphasize the true purpose of school. The list of intrusions continues as society purposes the school to do its bidding. Sports, occupational training, parenthood classes, health clinics, day care for student's children, family planning and even the provision of family planning supplies by some schools has taken the emphasis off of learning and substituted a studied common daily practice of living. Teachers and local administrators are tapped with assuring that the parents who register their children are in the proper school district. The whole idea of getting a better education is discouraged as students must be kept in possibly less desirable schools because there is no way to give all students an optimum public school experience. The social school is not offering exemplary education but almost any other function in lieu of academics and civility training.

Another authoritative principle is that education in the New School must be useful. This thirteenth principle is not pragmatic in the sense that education must have a useful function translatable in the near future into dollars, but useful in the sense that education must be able to inform and support learning and the intellect to the end of one's life. Any movement to reform that denies that learning and the ability to learn is not primary to any other good taught or modeled in the schools is drawn to that opinion by ulterior motives or unfortunate preconceptions of old school mediocrity. Much of learning cannot be correctly valued immediately. An exemplary education may not seem valuable now but has the power to deepen insights, to train minds to solve problems, to reflect critically on the past and to make sense out of a world that is more often in chaos and to require maximized capacity and practiced attention to reason. The mind that is trained to understand the world and the world of thought is going to be found not only more stimulated but also granted expanded options for interacting with the world in work and in leisure.

Finally, a true educational institution should protect education against the demeaning rituals and rote of the common culture without compromising the hard work of learning and teaching. True pluralism should be made real by each student and the school community as everyone is made aware of the essential dedication to combine efforts to educate each student maximally in an environment of mutual respect and responsibility, as well as develop the mental abilities in various studies with inquiry serving as the foundation for a critical learning methodology.

Chapter 4
Reconstruction and Society

Each generation is inclined to educate its young so as to get along in the present world instead of with a view to the proper end of education... Parents educate their children so that they may get on; princes educate their subjects as instruments of their own purpose.

- John Dewey, *Democracy and Education*

Public education failures will not be admitted to by reformers, theorists and politicos. In solving the problems of education, it is critical that any plan must be constructed apart from posturing, ideology, disruptive elements and conflict from interfering offices. The New School must be carefully and honestly analyzed for workable policy. The reconstruction of education, and that is no less than what is required to repair the leaky ship of public education, must strengthen broad academic interests and remove the debilitating reality of and concern for discipline, the malaise resulting from cultural intrusion and the arrogation of student rights issues. One methodological approach for school reconstruction could theoretically solve most if not all the problems incumbent on pedagogical architects. Any acceptable plan must allow for rapid response time for solving problems. Fixity may offer guaranteed success from the outset but may not account for sensibilities needed on a continuing basis. Establishing hard and fast rules may meet with legal resistance, but school working rules, to protect the school, must stand against changing problems. For up to date and locally established rules have the potential of being able to put out the fires of conflict and disruption before they start. The key is to replace rules as needed. Respect for law can be questioned on the basis that laws that are not enforced like spitting on the sidewalk, which once might carry a fine or jail time, have not been removed, that rules not removed when not needed merely gain law the reputation of irrelevance. School rules should not remain long after they have ceased to be useful and should be instituted quickly and fully to update defense of the school.

Integral to these plans is a defensive system of addressing school problems which will make it necessary to obviate rules to refresh implementation and provide new procedures as needed. The reality of education is that change in pedagogy is difficult at best, but, when bureaucracy holds the reigns tightly, policy and necessity generally allow little flex and freedom for needed change. Proposals presented here should be seen at least as a jumping off point for providing a workable authority for the school. Any new ideas on revamping the educational system that do not guarantee a local authority for the school will only be a pretense to improvement. Many school districts have paved the way for a sea change in public education through the charter school, which opened the door to local school autonomy and yet in most cases continued to dealing with the culture on its on terms. As in the main line schools this has and will invariably lead to educational disaster. Any new school must separate itself from the past and set in place defenses for education which will allow learning to be uninterrupted and undiluted by cultural intrusions.

The influences that are destroying the public school are attacks from without and within; they cannot be controlled from without. Problems of education must be solved within the protected environment of each school. The most hopeful reconstruction must take place sheltering the school from the society which would use it for its own purpose and by cultural standards that only certify mediocrity for the promise of academic excellence.

Internally the school must begin its rebirth from the ground up, not from the merely doable isolation of top down directives. Plans necessary to guard each school may vary widely as needs will vary, while basic safeguards may prove to be common to all. Like the Jumblies, the school historically has not been reasonably conjoined in thought and path. Each school must specify its own battle-plan defenses, its own appropriate and changeable defenses of placement and duration which would allow each school to meet all its challenges.

The framework for the New School, which can be applied to all schools without regard to socioeconomic and ethnocentric considerations, must fit pedagogy to the particular needs of the school, as a true democratic community where all students can be educated to the limits of their abilities. In the proposed New School, each student, each teacher, each local administration, should be given a part in the responsibility, indeed the privilege, of solving specific local problems which threaten educational excellence. National standardization of education could only lower goals for academic excellence. Making all academic goals comparable through country-wide testing would require mediocre standards. Academics would plunge in better schools and in schools denied true academic education pedagogy would only make moderate advances as the bureaucracy attempted to homogenize expectations in service to metrics. Each school's educational program would be seen as any other public school - one size fits all. Historicity would become one with the prevailing acceptable dogma of the times spread from ocean to ocean. Likewise other school subjects would take on the limits which would allow all students to achieve acceptable low-level proficiencies and a minimal understanding of the curriculum and the workings of their own minds.

Academics and democracy have served as ideals of American education: The New School would strive to provide for the real needs of the whole school and, at the same time, empower the individual student to excellence. With tolerance for all, while each student would be protected in holding personal values which can be challenged and reaffirmed in the spirit of the pursuit of true educational inquiry, ideals and beliefs should be on the table for democratic education to be truly applicable and communicative.

To take a fresh and more positive approach to public education, any change would have to give authority to the local school to decide how to manage and direct school activity. If each school were to be allowed academic and disciplinary autonomy, since all schools would be allowed to determined the details of school reconstruction within a proposed workable framework, there would be no excuse for districts to continue to promote elitist schools at the expense of those seen as less accepting or capable of higher levels of educational excellence. Cultural barriers to the academic community could be erased with reconstruction. The thought that a reconstruction could produce a supportive community of values and general communal care outside of the school is unrealistic in the short term. However, over time the graduates might have a positive net effect within their own particular areas of influence.

But can the goals of true public education be permitted while the cultural environment is hostile to all but the pecuniary advantages and the placement of school products, graduates, into leadership and labor? The answer, I believe, is yes. But the New School would have to offer true democracy, equal opportunity to all within the learning community. The courts, boards of education and college education departments have settled into political correctness which can only guarantee that school exceptionalism will never happen broadly and a denial that all schools have unsolved educational problems. Boards directing public schools want first and foremost a smooth education for their wards, few phone calls and frictionless operation of public schools with minimally unpleasant encounters with students, parents and the media. Exemplary educational is not at the top of their list of priorities. A successful public relations effort is preferable to a push for academic programs that work and produce an exemplary education for all.

To help in school reconstruction boards should actually become helpers in giving modern schools a chance to thrive with hands-on and experienced support for the school. Even, if well motivated to help, boards may not know what to do to help, but, if boards are not willing to get dirty to enable the schools to heroically teach and discipline students, then they should bow out of their policy-making role in the name of good judgment and out of consideration of the children impacted by careless and blind decision-making. The New School would call for the school staff, for the sake of the children, to stand in the door of the school in behalf of the realization of ideals of democratic education, make hard decisions about their school and not budge from the mission of providing maximal educational opportunity for all.

No governmental official is willing to risk conflict with the larger culture for this could be political suicide. The greater culture is ultimately the current authority in public schools where boards and district bosses do its bidding. Not challenging the methodology of education but the rights of individual students without a philosophy on which to base decisions more substantial than the wants of parents, legal organizations and students, many student-individuals become essentially unteachable finding their own unrestricted personal expression acted out on the public school stage, giving the limited fifteen minutes of fame that was promised. Much, if not all of this self-proclaimed individual authority takes its cue from a society which cannot say no to children and remote school administrators who are making or forcing decisions about students' lives based on a lie. That lie is grounded in the associative myth that all children can be successful no matter the curricular track and can go on to hope of undeniable fame. This makes it easier on the educational bureaucrat who may for a while avoid irate parents. The truth is that Johnny probably will not succeed if given a mediocre education and will not develop academic abilities if not held to hard work in study.

Each school must be empowered to bring authority to local education. In order to answer this issue of authority, it must be understood what the requirements are for the reconstructed school. Instructional foundation should be required of each teacher such that a philosophy of education both technical and propositional in nature should be a requirement for employment as each school must have a mission statement and an educational procedure which reflects a proven procedural philosophy. Mission statements, however, usually have no specific technical component and personal teacher philosophies are not discussed in most teacher training schools, since pedagogy is under system directive and very little in the way of educational direction arises from the individual teacher. There is no requirement for teachers to devise a philosophy or a summary methodology and proposed purpose concerning the art and science from which they draw their practice. This is not the fault of the teacher who may have naively embrace formal teacher education as fully preparative, but the boards that have screened prospective teachers and who are primarily concerned with the estimated managerial talents of teacher prospects may even find individual pedagogical theory an obstacle to fitting a prospective teacher into the present public system since a teaching philosophy may stand in the way of system policy goals or may seem too radical to be acceptable. Outside of meeting teacher certification and determining some general suitability for teaching, inquiries into a candidates prescient thoughts on education are not part of the usual job interview or even ongoing evaluation procedures. Teachers need to be given the responsibility in the New School to develop thoughts on the curriculum, broader challenges to methodology and the holism of curricular instruction. Teachers are the linchpin to the success of the New School and not the instrument of a clockwork educational system.

The public school system must turn and stand against a culture that will expect mediocrity while looking for a scape goat for school failure; it must defy cultural authority in favor of true education. Schools must have charge of their students and teach at a very high level without interference.

Chapter 5

Provision for a New School

> When the school introduces and trains each
> child of society into membership within such a
> little community, saturating him with the spirit
> of service, and providing him with the instru-
> ments of effective self-direction, we shall have
> the deepest and best guaranty of a larger
> society which is worthy, lovely and harmonious.
>
> - John Dewey, *The School and Society*

Based on past history, there is no reason to assume that the
problems concerning public education will somehow be remedied
by reform, and we cannot return to the traditional pedagogy of
even several decades ago. We must think of a New School for a
new time and see outside influences as a culture of usurpation in
which all that had value in the past can be replaced on the
assumption that all that is new is better. A New School, not held to
unanalyzed innovation, must be able to interface with the culture
on terms dictated by the school and, thereby, establish its own
authority. The reconstruction of the school must first start with a
sound school culture. Contemporary culture is, for the most part,
inert to purposive change, yet historically prone to succumb
incrementally to unanalyzed influence and absorptive of
innovation and constantly downgrading under the pressure of
exposure to the new. A tapestry of interwoven cultural elements
have been certified on the basis of the catch term diversity.
Diversity is sacrosanct and incapable of being rebuked for fear of
violating its unmeasurable toleration. Toleration, in its regard,
cannot be challenged but can itself repress through toleration
dogma to the exclusion of the ultimate melting pot of factions.

Toleration comes to mean the acceptance of any nuanced habituation of culture, while at the same time opposing strongly held positions of collective principle and authenticating often conflicting, often factitious beliefs. In the New School any designation of toleration must be vetted for the good of the school. There can be no toleration of disruptions, diversions or dissidence in building the New School. The conduct of students must be a central concern of the reconstruction process. Otherwise education will continue to be compromised by negotiations between children and school staff in deciding how education should proceed.

Whatever is decided about the nature of the New School, any concern that seems immediately pertinent and pressing to society that cannot be strictly judged central to academic education and worthy of the school's attention, must be jettisoned. The school must hold destructive student-individualism apart from the educational experience in order that students may develop both academically as well as socially under wise direction. The New School must be protected by disciplinary rules which can stand in reserve in undisputed authority to benefit all within the school environment. Discipline must be absolute within the New School. There should be no illusion that an appreciation of social pluralism will be entertained by student-individualists. Intelligent academic incorporation of social pluralism into the curriculum is supportive of and faithful to the letter of hard academics. Furthermore to maintain an open and even presence of such special interests in appropriate proportions, fair and balanced attention must be granted to each group as discussion arises in context to lessons. A protective function should be emphasized which would prevent group interests from drowning in their own self-absorbed exclusivity, foregoing any understanding of the rest of society and its cultures and working through any isolationism which might preclude students becoming vital contributors to cultural dialogue. This educational conversation must be possible in order to discuss deeply held beliefs but which should remain protected in the purview of each student.

To sidetrack disciplinary obstacles and any tendency to disunity through attempts at asserting group exclusivity, the New School must completely replace the existing weak and easily malleable old school. The school community, having no definable broad example, has been subject to idealistic musings, but it must become the New workshop in which a learning culture may be slowly rebuilt, a microcosm of learning and civility, by reintroducing into society examples of personal responsibility and care for all others. The idea that the young can be given insight into a democratic institution of cooperative sharing is problematic except for the use of heroic methodology to insure excellence in public education and a school staff taking full authority for the school. Communal practices must be instigated and maintained in reasoned authority, not in abstraction and loose affiliation. Just what is meant by community is important to a New understanding. Despite convincing real-life examples we may think of communities as associative aggregates made up of people who are tangentially positioned by coincidental yet mandatory interaction as in the workplace. Yet true community is vital and personal where transactions and interactions must be based on interdependence among those sharing commonalities. Our seeming nervous drive to mobilize and push ahead to new challenges without retaining true interactive interdependence among a common group of people is counter to the concept of finding deep and desired relationships in daily experience. Wc can not exempt collective learning which is the true format of most learning in life. Perhaps those relationships are not seen as important today, but any school system that disregards this interdependency is failing to capitalize on one of societies great democratic strengths, the ability to reason together, while, at the same time, giving individual opportunity for informed expression of his or her ideas in consideration of universal concerns which can be ultimately extrapolated to the school community.

Short of the occurrence of a major disaster, deep and broad relationships as those forged in the melting pot of the past may never be seen again and the impact of electronic communication may suffice for much of the interactivity within relationships. But one of the many victims of more distant associations has become the child. Picked up and moved every few years, in order to pursue the family fortune or the chance for better employment for parents, social stability of the home and academic progress of the student may suffer severely. There is no return to traditional understandings of community, nor even families with a singular focus on the good of their children. A society of associations has replaced broad relational communities. In the current public school today, true community seems impossible. A New School could structure the learning environment and emphasize that relationships can be real and deepened by the academic and civil discourse of inquiry and true and caring relationships within the school. This could offset the tendency to solitary existence which has been given the stamp of approval by default, while, at the same time, giving lip service to community. Relationships, as a result, have become devalued or ignored among students and school staff. The practice of school and curricular requirements are compromised by what Alexis de Tocqueville, the French writer of the nineteenth century, considered excessive familial centricity where the American family seemed to be more defensively unified against others than truly embracing the larger community. In the name of familial bonding, a family vacation or an impromptu daily outing with mom or dad on a school day may seem justifiable, but this is the stealing of educational group time, a theft from community in the name of family. The week day truancy, possibly by both parent and the child, each from their respective work, is nothing more than shirking duties for both the adults' work arrangements and the student's obligation to the school learning community. When students are shuffled between multiple and blended households in a often heroic feat of sibling management, which often results in disrupted study time and loss of academic focus, there is the compromise at the expense of the learning community. Much inattention to study has paralleled a dumbing down of academics and attendance requirements, while truant familial interests are becoming the accepted norm for an unapologetic, one might say, pseudo-community of individualistic family life. The school in complicity with this de-certification movement of the school community has become, to a greater extent, a licensing institution securing a right of passage for the individual student through an abstraction of numerical evaluations, while failing to seriously establish civil connectivity which can only be founded on reasoned inquiry and thoughtful respect. But school should be rightly constructed and seen as a community of academics with societal concern whose educated common purpose goes far beyond any merely unavoidable or nurturing associations of family as a place where individuals are educated en masse for the common good. In this way the New School could serve by unifying true academics and building true democratic community beyond the home.

A pretense of uncompromising service to the community cannot be allowed to disguise the current confused purpose of public education. Whether by maladministration or out of shear ignorance of purpose, those in charge of the old school must not stand in the doorway preventing the overdue reconstruction of a totally functional public school. The school must become its own authority in the democratic educational mandate. Society must be allowed influence in the school only under the wise authority of the school as it is dedicated to protecting the rights of all students both physically, emotionally and intellectually. The authority of the school should be assiduously guarded against mass cultural incursion by self-serving association, state or federal tampering or unanalyzed or political directives. America's dedication to extreme individualist rights promulgated by a culture that has asserted itself against the school, by design and by chance, must be pared back in order for reconstruction to begin a renaissance, a New School, but not by substituting yet another educational template on the school with formulaic approaches. Exemplary education can only be accomplished at the local level, one school at a time. The evidence is that not all schools have failed, and those that have, have not failed in the same way and for the same reasons and blanket procedural directives have never come close to fitting the school with needed policies for all schools.

The new school must recognize the importance of the environment in which the students learn. There should not be an untoward childish appeal to the school atmosphere for the schooling should represent an advancement on the tendencies of the young to remain immature and affixed to childish interests. The school is not the child's; it is the honored community of learners which continues in perpetuity among the school staff. As an arena for educational positivity of thought and action, each school must find its own expression of unswerving academics while building a community for learners. Cookie cutter approaches stand as hinderances to school integrity while sending the message that the framework of public education is primarily bureaucratic business as usual. The true democratic school is always the same, but always changing as it needs change and all the while being a wise judge and critic of the world outside its doors.

If the outcome of school-societal hybridization were to produce a more authoritative pedagogy, then the proof of pudding would be in the seriousness with which both teachers and students view the schooling process. The authenticity of schooling is not a parametric issue, it is part and parcel of what must be done in order to see that all students are educated, not just those who might blindly obey a mandate to learn, but also for those who must be held to educational opportunity despite their protestations.

Any understanding of academic school goals and how to attain them must be re-evaluated. Excellence does not need a test; it is self-evident. Tests that stand as standards are merely more icing on the unbaked cake of public education. Tests that require a level of competency that meets the required statistical standard are a denial of unbracketed knowledge. Taken as a whole the current formula for school failure constitutes the operational norm of a remotely driven, bureaucratically bungling and arbitrarily self-certifying model of an educational system which bares no authentic exemplary educational purpose. We must have in mind what we need education to be for all the students in all the schools. What we have in mind must be put to the charge and practice of teaching without apology or flinching from the set mark of excellence. Public education should be authentic in theory and in practice, both joined in mutually supportive and honest unity. That unity cannot be vested in the remote control of school boards dancing around public school but could only be truly reconstructed by radical means. Only by this turning of the system upside down would the Jumbled policies and wrong directions be extricated from the public schools.

Teachers must be given reasonable assignments in teaching. In the New School, they should be provided adequate time to grade and time to prepare lessons as well as being given reasonable numbers of students in each class so that interaction and inquiry can be maximized and made practical. Certainly under present classroom conditions a person having teaching credentials would be more likely to find an alternate career in something less destructive to both physical and mental health than teaching, in a system where there is less responsibility and more authority. Teachers need to be given the challenge of true academic excellence, to teach across the curriculum with authority. To meet the challenge of a more intelligent practice of teaching and develop a personal unified philosophy of pedagogy.

The New School must enable principals to run exemplary schools by providing the appropriate atmosphere for teachers to enjoin the task of modeling learning apart from the interfering irrelevance of political tampering. Time should be given for the principals to make the challenge clear both in respect to teaching and character modeling. Principals should have the ability to fire any employee who might compromise the mandate of building character by example, fail to generate cogent instruction, lack the effort to maintain continuity of lesson or fail to focus on an unwavering dedication to student involvement in the active inquiry of true education. Remote leadership has failed as it has looked first at the need for a certain teacher as one searches for a cog in a gear system - a machine. When a teacher disgraces the ranks, the policy first considers moving that teacher to another school. Only when the value of the cog is considered less than necessary by the board, based usually on cold scrutiny of the adverse impact on the school that retaining the teacher or staff member would have on system reputation, the teacher or staff member will be released from his or her position. The message is clear from the action of the remote authority: Character is less important than filling a vacancy. A negotiable solution to an employee problem and potential scandal may be weighed by how necessary the teacher may be in providing the immediate needs of the system. Such bureaucratic compromises are very often found as solutions and do not always result in firing. If the staff member is too important to fire or is not immediately replaceable then he or she may be moved to another school to avoid the local scandal and a repeat of problems, but the problems may rise again if the teacher is retained in another school sending the wrong message to everyone. The principle should have the power to remove the teacher for any infractions of discipline or lack of dedication to academic fervor. Rumor informs the students of scandals whereas staff may never know the details. The message is clear: hypocrisy, false values and board failure to act responsibly are detrimental to the learning community.

The principal, to properly evaluate the effectiveness of the school, should be a master teacher. I have seen this in the case of an elementary school principal by whom my wife was fortunate to have been supervised in teacher training and who she served under when her supervisor joined the system and became an excellent leader as a principal in the public system. My wife transferred to her school and stayed there until retirement. This principal would teach an elementary class within the school each day and discuss what she had done, and why, with the observing classroom teacher. Parents loved this principal. The teachers loved their principal and were eager to improve their teaching skills not by attempting to unscramble the abstractions of remote theoreticians but by learning at the hands of one who had taught all grades in a one-room school house in her youth. She understood the need for discipline and knew the true value of academics and did not compromise. It may come as no surprise that this fabulous pedagogic model was not one of the board of education's favorite principals, despite the fact that she was almost deified by the parents at her school, which provided high-level academics which in turn drew children of successful professionals to her. Her character, which was acknowledged by even her detractors, protected her against being removed from her position, which she would have gladly accepted if compromising principles were the requisite requirement for remaining in that position.

Boards of education stand in the way of effective reconstruction. It is the cumulative dereliction of duty by boards of education members fearful of their positions which have contributed to school failure. Reducing the role of boards while increasing the authority of each principal and each teacher would be a necessity in removing the heavy, awkward command of bureaucratic education. The New School would have a different look and a different leadership, a different size and organization. The tendency toward large schools and especially large class sizes makes exemplary education very difficult, but it is not the size of the school as it is the practice of the educational arts that determines school success or failure. Some modern public schools today may be small, but the greater trend has been to make them more economical by building schools to accommodate thousands of students.

No matter the organizational character of the school, the primary goal of the resulting New School plant is to teach children without unwanted interference from cultural influences. Careful scrutiny must be given to screen for influences that might be insinuated into the school environment as they are brought in by students, staff and through educational materials. Critical thinking developed through discussion must be the result of real issues of controversy, not by avoiding those issues. But to allow influences to pass into the school and be given passive acceptance without close, critical analysis of potentially adverse effects, would indicate that thinking critically is not an issue of life, certainly not of real concern to the school, and could actually be considered either the result of neglect or hypocrisy. A school-wide defense against the culture must be put in place in the New School to insure that it does not succumb to the character of the school it is meant to replace.

Attendance among other concerns must be defended. The law requires that the student attend school. It has been suggested to me by a former principal, that parents or students should have to pay for days missed. The funding of the school depends on the enrollment and attendance of its students, and this fine would offset the loss of funds by illegal truancies of students. Fines could also be leveed against parents who would remove their child from school for a family trip or a day of familial bonding. Raising the fine to an uncomfortable level might go a long way toward quenching some of the devaluing of schooling or at least cause parents to consider the budgetary issues which the school must address without full attendance. The school could use the money, no doubt, and the parent might be handed a lesson with the fine, a realistic cost for promoting the child's low regard for education. Not removing the child from classes for family affairs or parent-child days could be the most profitable lesson for both children and parents. The cost would pay for the makeup work required of the absent student under the supervision of Saturday teachers.

These are issues that will impact the organized and implemented New School. The New School must adopt a defensive posture against all that could and has happened to interfere with its educative purpose. In order to stand in defense of education it will be necessary for lawyers to come to the defense of the New School. Even in-school law enforcement officers, who have been in some schools for quite a while would be given broader powers. Defensive plans must be provided to the school so that the legal staff may systematically address student infractions instead of taking a measure from remote authority as the political barometer is applied to see what action to take against disruption. Disruption of a governmental institution anywhere else, that is, other than the public school, resulting in aggravated usurpation of authority, could result in an arrest and charges being filled. The school should be no different than other offices of the government in violations of the rights of the general citizenry. Violation of such laws in the school should be addressed such that behavioral issues are shown to be serious. This is a message, it could be argued, that has been neglected with children in the schools and has resulted in their being a loss of respect for public educational institutions, people that serve in those institutions and even the authority of law enforcement.

The New School must value education through academics that have not been compromised and dumbed down but dignified through a civil environment that teaches and learns respect for others. The school must be independent of the manipulation of politicos. A legal staff must be employed to hold back the assaults of the culture or even push back cultural encroachment. The New School should be dedicated to education and exemplary behavior. The New School should not reflect the whims and distractions of cultural influence. Defensive action, described in the next chapter, is proposed to quickly eliminate non-educative disruption and, thus, give the school the authority it was intended to exert in the name of the children it has a mandate to teach.

Chapter 6

Redoubts and School Protection

Where ever external authority reigns, thinking is suspect and obnoxious.

- John Dewey, *Reconstruction of Philosophy*

Sisyphus, in Camus' myth, was made by the gods to roll a large stone to the top of a mountain only to have it roll back down. This was his curse and was to be repeated over and over. Every school day the teachers and local administrators of most public schools roll the rock of modern pedagogy up hill. The onus bears down from essentially non-educative mandates of remote administration preventing public education from realizing its only dutiful and legal purpose: to educate all students. And this must be attempted against the erosive effect of societal incursions. Remote directives on how to teach and discipline are often politically and economically motivated. Handed down from on high by the "gods" under the heavy burden of uncertain school authority, the school staff often struggle beyond all reason to educate every student they can, while under the direction of superiors who will not admit to nor attempt to correct in any meaningful way the progressive futility that has been created. Ideologically and politically correct answers to any admitted school failure initiates a trotting out of yet another corrective reform program. The voyages of historic reform seem to arise from the same scenario: traditional school business as usual under conditions which often preclude universal learning. Like Theseus's ships, the complete replacement of theoretical planks of reform has historically resulted in the same failed ship of national public education which is re-launched year over year.

Each session runs aground in new issues of social immediacy, without proper bearing and resulting in pedagogy being blown to unproductive shores.

The "gods" seem to know little, or even care little, of the extreme dedication and energy required by local schools in fitting to the arduous task of pedagogy which are repeated again and again while only reaching a limited number of the students. This is an unending curse. It is time to seriously rethink the wisdom of continuing the subjugation of the public school to the expectations and limitations of the traditional Olympian overseers. Planning for a New School must draw on all times: learning from the past, attending to the present and looking to the future while dedicated to making real the "public good." But this cannot not be accomplished when efforts to do so are cobbled together remotely as teaching is weighted down with essentially administrative-protective policies. The question that must arise is more foundational than that of the waste of teacher energies and untaught students. What exactly does the community outside the school actually have to offer that is vital to an academic education? Are not the tools of academics the foundation for learning of the world around? Certainly what ever the world outside the school has to offer educationally must be subordinated to that of a consideration of requisite academic inquiry, to balanced observation and experiencing broad history with wisdom. Naively allowing the culture a free pass into the school has been much of the problem that public schools have faced in their long history as the victims of bureaucratic abuse. The school can become a wise critic of society and learn from it, and, if it is given the protection from the usurpation of the time and skills needed to arrive at an educated understanding of society, it should be better prepared to deal with the problems associated with the looming authority of community outside the school.

There is, therefore, the issue of bringing community into the discussion of what schools should be. This would seem, in many ways, to be putting the baby back in much of the dirty bathwater rather than to be tossed out for clean. Defenses should be put in place to remove the obstacles to academic teaching and learning and reasoned civility, which in these regards there seems to be no realistic high values attached in the broader society. Instead the tendency has been, it seems, to rush to summarily open the floodgates of the culture into the school. The local school should set the agenda and not the outside, since the local school and its staff of teachers and administrators have to face the often insurmountable daily problems and ultimately receive the blame for their inability to act on remote authority's summons, or improve education on the direction by cultural mavens who might wish to get behind the school but whose inclinations are counter to good academic policy or are as remote in understanding as the gods of pedagogy that divine the problems and offer failed solutions for the school. Community support may be well-meaning but invariably shows little knowledge about instruction and curriculum and specializes in non-educational policies and programs. Reform rather than creation from the ground up is all that is handed down by the remote gods.

Protecting the New School from the cultural and administrative insipidity should be part of a school replacement dialogue. Correctly understood the intent and the outcome of proposing a New School is, in all ways, to attempt to educate without the dilution of educative purpose and tenor. The larger culture seems unwilling to demand academic schools as educational diversions from outside the school compromise education's capacity with no willingness to curtail its effects. The societal understanding, which is often contradictory and foments controversy, can never inhere in academic education, since it is incapable of being represented without being ruled by emotional and proprietary issues.

Teachers together with local administration may have the answers for the New School. If they do not, then certainly those that hardly grace the classrooms of teachers and confer openly with local principals, cannot help. The old school directives too often obstruct teachers and the schools in finding an effective approach to the teaching of children. The new school must find productive methodologies to rebuild, re-experience and refortify a new public school, a New and worthy vessel.

The school should not have to apologize for setting academic and civil standards despite the remote administration's fear that hard standards might leave the public displeased and could endanger re-election, re-appointment or future political aspirations. Parametric authority - boards, judges, legislators and executors - if the "public good" were their true concern, should be spokesmen for the teachers, serving the teachers and local administrators, instead of trying to protect personal currency and a hierarchical system that is moribund: for these have no first-hand knowledge for correcting school deficiencies. The needs and defense of education must be determined by each school for each school from within the school. With a New School there must be a method for defending academics and civility from the culture outside the school and the student-individualist culture inside the school. Any such defense must provide an unwavering policy; it must derive its reason for existing from local, immediate or projected needs, and it must exist under local school policy founded on the best judgment of the school staff. There must be a stern warning through consequences leveed against those that would attempt non-educational intervention and disruption. As in battle, the school needs to provide defenses that protect against compromising attacks. And as aggression shifts to a new flank, then a new defense must be rapidly deployed. In battle without a quick defensive strategy, the war may be lost. In war time and on the battle field such a defense may be termed a *redoubt*, a defense by which a necessary stronghold can be built as a quickly assembled barrier to ward off attack. Such a strategic battlement is only defensive. Redoubts may be as numerous as defenses are needed in war. Since they are not necessarily fixed in design, they may be erected and taken down as needed and changed or amended as the nature of attacks change. However, as in war they have consequences when a breach is attempted. The consequences for attack too would be the responsibility of the school to judge.

In the New education wars, each school must erect its own defensives against attack. Because of the need for rapid deployment of defenses or redoubts, it is essential that each New School identify and provide efficiently and peculiarly appropriate resistance for its own defense. Defenses handed down from remote administration would be too broadly applied, to all schools, possibly too slow in deployment and almost certainly inappropriate to at least some schools. The only redoubt that would meet the need of efficient protection for a school would be those erected to on-site attacks by those who have actually experienced rebellious defiance, who actually know first-hand of what the attacks consist and what might be done to curtail them.

An immediate, local plan for restoring true individual freedom to *all* in the school community is to be had by establishing redoubt goals which can guarantee school authority in academics and citizenship for all students. Redoubts can protect the school. The history of truly educational and consistent purpose and unending and unevaluated reform has given very little to progress in education. The child-centered system of pedagogy has failed, yet hangs on in the practice of those who seem to truly care for the school community but are helpless to see it profit from their actions and intent. Absurdity and reason have been hybridized in absurd policies and programs. A story attributed to Albert Camus, the French-Algerian existentialist, tells of a psychiatrist who while observing a patient insanely fishing in a bathtub asks if the fish were biting. To this the patient responded that the doctor must be a fool for he, the patient, was fishing in the bathtub. The absurdity of modern and historical American education is that fishing for educational excellence, no matter how true to technical appropriateness, like using the right tackle, can only produce positive results if the environment is also appropriate. Like the bathtub the modern public school is inappropriate for hooking excellence.

Reason has not as with technique told us that we are ultimately constrained by this unworkable school environment. We must give to reason first, then redoubt against further technical failures in the school according to experience. Let us reconstruct the school, realistic to the task and proximal needs. Let us help, through reasoned and redoubted education, to move our students from the base of the mountain of Sisyphus toward its acme as academic education is allowed to flourish and the learning community is made manifest. Educational policy should give our teachers and local administrators Promethean confidence; it should take away the Protean disguises of modern educational directives; and it should remove the Sisyphean rock of redundant futility. The historic failure of public education is an absurdity and totally avoidable. The New School should defend against such folly. A new school cannot be built, until any previously hailed and failed programs are removed from practice. All traces must be removed for imposing good policy or bad policy will only taint the product. Redoubts can then be installed once the system has been purged of counterproductive policies and damaging cultural preferences.

Redoubt proposals, if they could withstand litigation, could not only gain authority for beleaguered public schools but could justify a formative public school pedagogy. As a result of being charged with sweeping accusations of incompetence, teachers as a group need for their own sanity, if for no other reason, to hear the truth about public education in order to keep a firm grip on reality. They are labelled by the media and on occasion their own boards of education, that they are not all properly and effectively teaching their students. Teacher colleagues and myself fantasized of having one day a year to tell the truth about the way that education was being manipulated and the questionable reasoning required to justify the procedural mandates that we were required to meet. That day, appropriate to the task, would be April first, April Fool Day. We would tell the truth that we knew and following the chorus of verities, would then as our minds would be guarded for another year, return to a deceptive practice by which we struggled to make a difference in the education of the young baring the weight of what we cannot say or completely fulfill in our practice. And although we were only a Greek chorus to the drama of the educational undoing, we would hope to see the day in which all students could find an education unrestricted by bureaucratic will.

Redoubt strategies, would go a long way to provide the the reality of educational practice and thereby civil and academic education could be for the first time addressed. It would challenge the practice of universal directives, or at least remote practice, by using specific redoubts to avoid that which threatens education in each school, by finding redoubts which would address specifically and immediately those forces adversely affecting the school. Only reconstructing the school with appropriate and defensible safeguards will bring America its first true democratic school. A productive and lucid approach to reconstruction where issues threatening the school's ability to teach are averted allowing the pursuit of academic excellence, plurality in more than name only and civility among all within an ordered community, could help usher in the New Democratic School. If there is a risk in reconstructive redoubts, then it can be no more risky than the fall out of failed reforms that have been allowed to intervene for so long. A public school must be erected which will permit the building of community in perpetuity to insure the concept of community will not be lost even if the school must hold up in seclusion to pass along the tools of thought and letters. Redoubts as a working policy in reconstruction could help the school become a truly democratic institution. Perhaps the New School may take a chance to help in returning the concept of "character" to the common school's communal consciousness and maybe even to a common public. The school may be a laboratory for modeling the hopes of civilization, which much of modern life seems to have forgotten. Lack of courage, the fear of taking chances in the pursuit of an honored and honorable school, this is the public school legacy which must be replaced.

The type of redoubts that might be needed by any particular school might be concerned, say, with dress restrictions. Mandatory uniforms trump uniformity-of-dress policies which are prone to disputation as such judgements are impossible to explicitly prescribe standards among different dress attire. If the school needs to create this type of redoubt, the arguments for and against would not be about the students right to wear anything that was desired, but, since all would wear uniforms in good faith, one distraction from learning and divisive individual or group identification could be averted. Any perturbation to the process of teaching would not be permitted on the authority of redoubts which each school adopts. The authority of redoubts may also be extended as proactive measures in anticipation of future unacceptable intrusions. All redoubts on the battlefield are preventative measures, those in the classroom and the halls of the school should be no less preventive in nature. Legal opposition should be deflected by asking whether the presumption of injury to the schooling process is important enough that a school defense, by redoubts, if it could be successfully put in place, could insure that each student obtain an exemplary education. Would a positive outcome justify objections to protective school rules?

It is not that redoubts would be enforced without advising all concerned of their implementation. All redoubts would be clearly communicated to parents and amended as necessary, and, if modified, then detailed changes would be described to parents. A list of redoubt controls would be given to parents and submitted to the New School lawyers, more of which will be forthcoming. Redoubts could even defend against damage to the school community by instituting an honor code, a mainstay of private institutions. If this is not a consideration for proposing a better education then why are parents willing to pay for their children to attend an expensive private school while still having to pay for a public education they do not use? Is it possible that the private schools are doing something right? Well it does not appear that the public system believes that to be true, or public schools would be prescribing mimetic programs and restrictions on students as private schools are known to do.

For any redoubt so conceived in real consideration of known disruptive elements or even the inkling of disruption, the decision to do nothing or to try to walk around the problem at hand, would, by reconstructive rule, not be permitted, and each defense would be targeted only to expedite clear and decisive action. No problem, as bureaucrats tend, will be subject to tabling or expanded beyond or diminished below any particular redoubt's purpose. Redoubts would not be given the familiar bureaucratic wink. Thoughtful understanding would guide appropriate and immediate action.

In addition to legal protection of the school and its staff, additional redoubts may be justified that take a defense stand against the community or culture outside the school. Legal proceedings may need to be brought against those extra-educational forces which threaten the educational success of the young. For instance, if an employer allowed a student to work excessive hours, then the employer should be brought to court by school lawyers who, on the basis of a current redoubt, would determine if the student had been taken away from studies by the student's employer, that is, has he or she, with the consequences of a lifetime, abused the student by interfering with life-long opportunities. It is possible that even a curfew lawsuit could be brought to trial by school lawyers in order to insure that children are able to obtain a good education when parents and employers seem not to care if the student gets a opportunity to be educated.

Redoubts may arise over the appropriateness of vocational education to an exemplary education for all students. We now pass on the trades taught within the school as the right training for some students, while for many it precludes a better life that could more surely be had through academics. Due to parental failure or laziness on the part of the student who by following the work curriculum could almost surely be fated to lead a life that is met with intellectual and vocational dead ends, redoubts, as each school decides necessary, may be put in place that insure against the loss of educational potential by removing vocational training from a school's curriculum.

Redoubts are less about jobs, cars, disruptive clothing, and group oppression than about an intelligent control of the learning environment where a perpetual attempt to provide all students with an exemplary education is possible. Athletics have severely overreached their importance, have been given as a reason for attending school and as a measure of school involvement. It may be necessary, depending on the school, to eliminate sports programs, if academic success does not concurrently meet muster. Instead of holding each individual to a grade-standard restriction in order to participate in sports, it may be necessary to suspend athletics until the school is able to meet overall academic and behavioral standards, then guardedly consider reinstating athletic competition with the stipulation that if suspected of compromising academics or community, it will once again be dropped from school activities. Athletics is only an example. The emphasis on athletic competition to the exclusion of exemplary education can and often does derail academic expectations for the young as they contemplate unrealistically an almost non-existent chance of making athletics a life-long profession. Each public school would need to determine if it were necessary to build redoubts against sports. Any argument to the effect that both academics and athletics can coexist, when the former is not exemplary, is patent dishonesty. Schools need to be able to protect athletically-minded students from unreasonable dreams and train them in the pursuit of academic awards. Although the opportunities in degree-based professions may not be as profitable as the higher-paid professional athletes, there is no confusion over whether academics is being promoted as a winner-take-all gamble, while sports aspirants have a statistically small chance of participating in college programs and even less of a chance of going on to participate at the professional level.

If a redoubt defensive system were to amazingly find acceptance in the school, it would have to be defended by every legal means when challenged. The system, in most instances, will be attacked for no other reason than to guarantee Johnny's right to self-expression and unfettered freedom. Considering the adverse effect that Johnny could have upon the student that wants a challenging and academic education, by all common reason, the unrelenting fight for the self-expression for all surely super-cedes Johnny's rights. Only teachers, administrators and parents focused on the child's real needs can defend everyones reasonable rights, even Johnny's, and only those in the school, working with the students, planning and teaching lessons, can provide a balanced view of student's rights.

Certainly redoubts cannot make students do what is best for them, they only make it easier to do the right thing within a controlled environment thus eliminating many if not most counter-productive influences. Redoubts cannot be perfect, they cannot be entirely appropriate for all sensitivities, but as long as redoubts are not injurious to the child, managing all students is beneficial. Through close care, redoubts can communicate clear guidelines for behavior, academics, motivation and expectations. The key to redoubt success must be to identify the impediments to learning and citizenship and erect redoubts in defense of the child.

We must stabilize the lives of a generation of young learners. Those factors which destroy public education or give it secondary importance beneath cultural imperatives are to be defended against. When academic education is appropriately advanced on wise advice, no opposition should be offered by reasonable people. Establishing and changing redoubts as needed may be seen as experimental, but school reconstruction requires insight, action, planning and continual reevaluation on the part of teachers and local school administration. Radical redoubts, it is safe to say, would not work in most all of the schools and districts in the present cultural climate. Remote administrations would not concede to political issues that might stand for the betterment of schools for students and relinquish their authority and power to control, even for the good of the schools and their students. Attempts would be met with heavy opposition also from parents and litigious watch-dog organizations who feel that the destructive nature of their overreaching litigious influence is only making the old school better.

If there is any resentment toward the redoubt process so be it, but failure to defend the school is unthinkable, and reforms portend only further failure. Without a deliberate and drastically surgical pruning of a top-heavy school bureaucracy with perennial goals, actors and problems, more reforms will follow failed reforms while children suffer interminable unproductive experimentation. Redoubts must not be seen as draconian by measuring an unacceptable loss of individual freedom, but, rather, the advancement of a learning community, a guarantor of democracy for all. There is a better way to deliver and protect education for America's children. We may change the approach; the rigor of curricular content but disciplinary freedoms must never be compromised unless all profit from the restraints. The fruits of progressive education have fallen to the ground again and again and not far from the tree. Redoubts can quickly bring workable, exemplary public schooling to fruition. The aggressiveness with which appropriate defensive and educational methodologies may be employed will depend on the particular school, its endemic community and its ability to grasp the positive significance of the weblike daedal system of redoubts, which may circumvent problems before they arise. We will probably not change society through the school but we can expect to keep society's detrimental influences from continuing to prevent excellence in public education and hopefully export into the larger community intelligence and civility even as it is being lost in greater effect.

Redoubt cannot answer all the threats to the school. The problems that in the short term or even long term that may not be resolved by redoubt defenses, can grow with litigation on behalf of the schools to find a proper learning environment against those that would not value its full work of educating the mind and heart. The home and the broader culture outside the school will raise to gale force disapproval at any suggestion of reconstructing education. But the school must defy culture. Culture is not infallible, not even consistent or self-judgmental. Bad influences and ideas in the general society are ignored or tacitly replaced by a new influence, an influence usually no more closely examined than the unanalyzed influence which the new replaces. The replacement with redoubts could prove no more destructive to school culture than its waffling predecessor. It is likely that even with time and temper it may be impossible to change culture, never changing or repenting of its failures. But in the mean time, students will get an education in a properly reconstructed New School which addresses the understanding of reason and thought, and is better able to separate what is real and truly profitable from that which is superficial and borrowed or even damaging.

Chapter 7

Organization of the New School

I would make education a pleasant thing both to the teacher and the scholar. This discipline, which we allow to be the end of life, should not be one thing in the schoolroom, and another in the street. We should seek to be fellow students with the pupil, and should learn of, as well as with him, if we would be most helpful to him.

- Henry David Thoreau,
Uncommon Learning

Thoreau was a school teacher who saw the student in idealistic terms. He did correctly understand that what we demonstrate as discipline in the schools should be consistent with the "street," although his version of discipline, a Romantic version, would differ greatly from that of strict disciplinarians. Thoreau saw that teachers should be learners like their students, yet experience has taught those who observe and listen that we cannot share authority among students and school staff without losing school authority to teach, learn and discipline. Thoreau's idea that teacher and student should be learners in the classroom is admirable but education as a "pleasant thing" is not so convincing especially when the necessity for discipline and hard study tell another story.

But how would a plan for public school excellence be constructed using redoubt methodology to control the educational environment, providing firm but fair disciplinary policy for guaranteeing the ability to provide challenging academics? The school purpose would initially address the recognition of the particular practical problems faced by the school. Demographics, ethnicity and student-individualist culture should be carefully screened by school leadership, the teachers, guided by the principal, in order to provide the necessary series of restraints peculiar to that school. The goal is to oppose any forces or factors which would preclude an excellent educational experience for its children.

Trust in classroom instruction and curriculum will grow with the use of redoubts which will direct uninterrupted attention to teaching and learning. Calls that brand defense as coercive are nothing more than an attempt to preserve territorial acquisitions held jointly by detached leadership and a rebellious student-individualist faction. Redoubts would hold to a determined local authority preventing incursions by the attacking opposition. Redoubts can be made to stand against threats to exemplary education from within or from outside each school.

In the best and worst of public schools there are those for whom education is a priority, academics is sacrosanct and the communication of life changing wisdom is eruptive. Remote authority, boards and governmental legislators and executors, should be spokesmen for the teachers as they serve teachers' every need. Additionally, lawyers would serve teachers in tying up the litigious public and opportunistic bottom-feeders in their relentless push to academic and civil disconformity or those scratching at school authority in order to empower directionless individual freedoms for student-individuals. These opportunists can be stopped in their determined efforts to see public education drift and sink in its leaky boat of authority.

Schools must have their independence from the regressive programs of reformers as well as powerful spectators on the shores. Dubious solutions trickle down through the system while no hard rulings persist: every rule is meant to be bent or broken. Remote verdicts may result in the inappropriate edicts which may only limit the teacher and local administrators ability to deal effectively with problems. Those who attack the school system are placated in a policy of avoidance whereby controversial issues are defused or set aside. There is no guarantee of personal integrity among an authority which finds professional opportunity and conflict in their quasi-binding judgments. Local school management can not be expected to flourish where direct interaction with problems is not possible. Teachers, as trustees of America's public school children, are charged with the job of being models of integrity and behavioral character, on site, satisfying the characteristic requirement that they be personally dedicated to students and the school community. Their efforts are very often scuttled when their authority is challenged and never being able to immediately solve a problem without contacting the highest leadership.

Principal sets the tone for teachers to enjoin the task of modeling learning. Principals must make the challenge clear both in respect to teaching and character modeling. Based on principals not finding sufficient indications of either, they should have the ability to fire unworthy staff without bowing to the remote leadership. Any employee who compromises the mandate of building exemplary character by example or by not teaching hard academics should be removed from the school under the authority of the principal alone. Teachers along with the principal must work together to set standards of behavioral for each school. Benign authority must rest with the principal. The principal should be a master teacher. To be the head principal one should be versed in virtually all the subjects required of the teachers in that school. Today's principal is not required or allowed this necessary credential but is made, no matter the inclination to academics, just as each teacher, into a political pawn for every force in government and the public. For most principals there is no time to directly devote to the core purpose of education. The job of managing the school is usually under the local reins of multiple administrators each with the responsibility of quelling some facet of public, parental or student-individualist uprising. But what if all school teaching staff could give all their effort to making education itself better instead of having to sort out myriad events that threatens school policy meltdown ? Public education would, if for no other reason, improve, if the common purpose for all school staff could become the undisputed and ultimate education of all children.

If the school is to become a true community of learning and learners, non-educational issues must be abandoned. Despite the controversy, it must be said that collective bargaining units are disruptive to the school purpose and become a wedge between the local administration, who are usually not members of a union, and the teachers who in most cases are. With new evaluation procedures in place, a new layer of conflict has been added. Local administrators are now being evaluated based on not only their performance in running the school, but, as a part of the process, the teachers' evaluation scores of administrators. This is driving a wedge between the local administrators and the teachers. Administration should always be ready to help teachers without the divisiveness created conflicting accountabilities and loyalties. Education of students should be held to higher standards than individual evaluations.

The system is becoming less student focused and given more to personal attention which presents an imposing obstacle to the running of a school. This is an unfortunate influence and is a threat to the dynamics of the educational process. Any influence that targets the student as exclusively individual is detrimental to the school purpose. Any influence, whether outside the local school, handed down by remote administration or collectively bargained by labor organizers, that is not educational, in the strictest sense, should have absolutely no elevated position in the school activities. Discipline cannot be a major part of the school's concerns. The emphasis needs to be taken off of personal aspects of communication and placed exclusively on educational policy.

Much of the service sector of the board function would be contracted out so that insurance, bookkeeping and most other services could be written off the school budget for lower salaries and perks including retirement costs. This would also have the benefit that school policy would not be controlled by ancillary workers qualified for non-educational duties. All operational decisions for individual school policy would arise from within each school and would be final. Any parent or organization that might want to bring challenge to the authority of any academically or disciplinary redoubt must be willing to defend such a counter proposition at risk of being found accountable for assuming the financial risk encountered before the court.

Discipline would be handled by an in-house law enforcement officer. Any problems that arise in the New School would not result in drawn out meetings of parents ranting about the redoubt policies. Any problems arising beyond the teachers' ability to work out a satisfactory resolution of discipline would be assigned to the school marshal. Any second disciplinary offense would be turned over directly to the school marshal for arrest and prosecution. School officers have been installed in school districts for decades, but their function has been merely to deal with students in situations that have clearly gone over into the area of criminal violation, usually involving drugs or violence. The proposal here is that any situation found to be an unresolvable disciplinary violation, being usually defined as a second offense on the part of the student individual, would be taken on by the law enforcement representative and resolved through the juvenile or criminal justice system. This would insure that student disruption would not derail the attempts of the school to carry out its mission to teach and model civility, since disruption would be considered a prosecutable event. The marshal would function like any other law enforcement officer who responds to a breach of the peace resulting in arrest and prosecution. The marshal would retain absolute authority for disciplinary issues which for school law breakers would result in being placed in a cell, provided in the officer's official office on the school property, until such time that the suspect can be brought to a permanent jailing facility. A true zero-tolerance policy to handle disciplinary infractions would be constructed for the protection of the school community and its legal right to give each student an education.

It must seem that this is a drastic measure to take against children. The days of corporal punishment are gone. Whether this was an effective deterrent to misbehavior is endlessly discussed and will never be agreed on. Physical abuse seems to be addressed more often today than in past times. Whether instances of physical child abuse were as prevalent in the past is not known, since it was not talked about as openly as today and there were not always laws that were enforced against such treatment of children. All of this being considered, there is no universally acceptable way to use corporal punishment for disciplinary purposes today. However, using the legal system, as it is appropriately used in the world outside the school, students and parents could gain a clear understanding of the legal justice system before the training wheels are removed and the students graduate into the work-a-day world. Resultant court records would be reserved for the future but could be accessed on release to potential employers as are grades when authorized by the student upon graduation. Graduation, apart from long-term incarceration of students for more aggressive infractions of the law, would be an absolute legal requirement. There would be no GED bypasses or frivolous home school dodges. Many home schoolers are better taught than many in the public or private systems, but some parents have sheltered their children from the purview of the public system and not given a rigorous education to their children. This must stop. The children that are not educated and civilized will become, more or less, wards of the state and drag down the system and ultimately not be full contributors to society.

And those students that recurrently enter the legal system can be passed onto a bunk school in which the students work for part of the day and study the rest. It is here called a bunk school since troubled students would be retained in the school, would sleep and eat there until there term was finished at which time the students could be returned to the regular school and their homes.

Each school would have a lawyer who would remain on site for the marshal as a sort of receptionist in the marshal's outer office. Any disciplinary issues would be addressed by the officer with routine first offenses being dealt with as a written warning with subsequent disturbances resulting in mandatory incarceration. The school lawyer would supply litigious parents, with the proper papers for bringing suit against the school or summons for those parents who defy or contribute to the student's interference with school rules leading to prosecution. The school lawyer would also be able to set a trial date, having access to court dockets as well as a schedule for availability of the board lawyers, in order to expedite proceedings, if the parent wished to pursue the issue of legal objection in court. Municipalities might want to set aside a juvenile court to handle just school charges. With the school lawyer able to collaborate in setting court dates for parents declaring to file suit, the courts may more easily expedite hearings. Based on charges, the lawyer may supply information concerning any civil or criminal charges that might be brought against an accused student-individualist. Judges and jury may even find space in the school grounds for the trials, in an attempt to set an example as well as expedite the process of judgements and consequences. School courts could be held at night on school property near the homes of litigants. This would also serve to tie discipline to judgments on the authority in dispute, the school grounds, on which the law was broken.

The school lawyer would interface as an adjunct to the board lawyers allowing an accurate and detailed statement of charges to be prosecuted and may even be responsible for aid in brief preparation. Resultant successes in new positive rulings for teaching handed down by the courts may be used in forming New School policy directly in local court victories for the school and by extension to all other public schools. A consortium of school law attorneys, employed by public schools could flood the courts with authority rendering court successes that could establish the public school as a viable, serious and effective institution. Such progress would offer the hope to all public schools both by legal precedent building and supporting a extra-school defense through aggressive adjudication and, in time through trials, the public school could win legitimate authority. A federation of school lawyers, one would hope, would win ultimately from precedent in working together, across this country, the necessary authority to teach all students while producing a truly democratic and authoritative educational system. It is only the judiciary which portends to remove the obstacles that society has allowed to intervene in public education and that has continued to weakened the school.

Each school would give time early in the day for teacher planning time and extended time for grading written work which would constitute the bulk of assignments. Students would also have preparation time during teacher work periods. This would augment the homework time that would be found on the part of the student under penalty of law. Teachers would be the nervous system of the New School. The curriculum would result from teacher input based on uncompromising academic goals and planning. Some testing could be even outsourced to non-public school graders, in order to give the student a more objective evaluation as well as giving teachers more time to prepare for classes. The responsibility to learn would fall squarely on the shoulders of the student and the parents to learn without restrictions. Students would attend not just physically but would give unrestricted mental approbation to the new school system's attempt to equip each for a life that does not limit academic potential or the fruits of their contribution to their community and country. Direct advice and counseling by professionals invited into the schools from higher education and other distinguished professional areas would measure the educational excellence attained by students for the work they propose to enter after college. This will tend to remove most dreamlike beliefs that many students tend to hide behind that by not studying and not learning there is still a clear avenue for success and higher academic degrees.

The new school would be not just a better school for all students but a better school for society. Both interests are served when the student gets the best possible academic education. Failure to attend would result in stiff fines, probably best leveed as a special school tax or added to local property taxes. The law for compulsory attendance optimistically would be extended over time by school law suits to include an understanding of compulsory learning. Students of special needs, found to be a part of the small contingency unable to proceed with rigorous training, would receive an exemplary education to the limits of the child's ability. Those refusing an education would be considered for the alternative bunk schools with release being contingent on adequate work and study evaluations.

The attention to schedules, to efficient use of time, the organization of a productive mind, levels of academic inquiry, and the consideration of self-educational dedication, may be addressed by redoubts within the New School reconstruction. There would be a necessary degree of regimentation, phased in over time, necessary to intensify student's focus on academics and good citizenship. Besides receiving, as in the middle of the last century, a general citizenship grade or a conduct grade, since in the New School such a consideration would be no longer needed, the student would be given a response grade, based on discussion, use of Socratic-styled and reasoned communications with both teachers and students, and the development of powerful, appropriate and sensitive argumentation. This would be the new measure of sociability. Student education would be both truly academic, yet with a social conscience. If social expectation are found unacceptable, then varying degrees of structure could be imposed ranging from detention by the legal justice system to a term or more in a bunk school.

What has first been purposed for reconstruction is revolutionary, a near impossibility in today's climate of bureaucratic organization and fear that the public would see giving children an exemplary education as burdensome and coercive. Call this a fool's dream, a deconstruction of public education, but this New School could stop school failure in one broad unified sweep. It would guarantee, I believe, if such a system could be established, say, through the charter school movement, a way to protect education from the cultural challenges that the old school struggles against and which prevents a universal and serious undertaking of academic education. But short of storming the boards of education, there would be no voluntary self-diminution by board members and certainly not by the underlings which add to layers of remoteness. For those intent on educating America's youth without restricting student intelligences, this is devoutly to be wished. If the New School came about, how would this plan of public school excellence be reconstructed, if it could? The redoubts would be put in place to defend educational requisites as opposition arose. Yet the naysayers' cries from the shore would still be unceasingly critical of any attempt to change or, should it be said, establish a non-dysfunctional educational system. If these calls are meaningful, then let them show that their theories for developing a true democratic school have worked broadly and not in special cases, special districts or demographics, but rather across the breadth of the public school system. If success, and this is the challenge, cannot be shown in each and every school, success cannot be claimed.

Ideally the reformers need to bow out and let education, led by local school communities, take a responsive and defensive redoubt position on the wisdom of a knowing, caring and wise local school staff. Some redoubts would succeed in defending the school and some will not. Redoubts should not overstay their effectiveness. Teachers and administrators would need to embrace legal school counsel to defend against the suits which would be brought against the New School. Questioning the right of a school to challenge individual student's "rights" at any level will result in suits. This tendency must be opposed at all costs in the courts.

The New School organization would provide fewer layers of accountability, less time spent in conference with parents since all rules would be fixed for their useful duration and stand as non-negotiable directives thus solving the disciplinary side of the educational problem. For we have schools today which are struggling for the authority to teach and spend most of their time and personnel energies addressing non-educational issues for which the public school cannot find the authority to overcome. Bringing law enforcement into the schools with the weight of legal authority will help bring the discipline problems under control for every public school. There is also the real consideration that the public school has not been, in reality, if not even in theory, the school for all children. The New School will finally be able to give every student equal treatment, both in academics and in discipline, producing a true democratic and civilly responsible institution. This must be addressed in any consideration of reconstruction or even reform programs. To do less is to add reform to reform and to recreate the same problems of school authority that have plagued education for over two centuries. A new responsible, democratic and academic school is the only answer that can be pressed to bring the public school out of its dilemma and give it academic authority.

Chapter 8
A Worthy Vessel

Every moment instructs, and every object; for
wisdom is infused into every form.

- Ralph Waldo Emerson, Essays

Domestic education is the institution of nature;
public education, the contrivance of man. It is
surely unnecessary to say, which is likely to be
the wisest.

- Adam Smith, *The Theory of Moral Sentiment*

A worthy public school system will not allow its schools to drift into the disruptive and dark storms of cultural predilection on the advice of remote observers on the shore. With thoughts of academic school success but with hands that are given primarily to social concerns, the current school system leadership is unable or unwilling to stand against society's diverse and divisive entanglements and, therefore, unable to give sole attention to academics and an unsullied school learning community environment. A board of education, so reconstituted, or school system leadership must be made worthy of its charge by serving the school and its staff, defending all the school staff while making the way safe for academics against pragmatic opposition.

The new school must focus on academics not testing, on the private and public aspects of the learning school. High leadership of the schools seems to consider only the school and society in some grand abstraction which in real terms they are not able to understand having little to no contact with the practical aspects of education and are unable to prescribe for the dissolution of degrading social influences that persistently derail the school effort. Their programs and policies are arrived at without direction and insight into school purpose and fall under the weight of politically weighted issues. Among all the failures of the current system, what must a valid system of public education consist; what must characterize a worthy new school?

The worthy school must be unified in purpose not as the Jumblies with heads and hands in conflict but in a thought-action unity. What our mind sees as academic must not be put to the test of society's drive to solve all problems through social action, instigated in order to provide for the whole child. The worthy school is a learning community in which learning community members must generate meaningful education through academic communal discourse. Introducing a social proxy into the school can do nothing more that produce a social education, that oxymoronic designation, which equates education with building community apart from hard academics. Education is about hard work and hard study while reforms have only offered frameworks for failure. Reformers preserve their own positions and try to find only reform programs that promote their own ideologies with the least amount of professional risk. They never look beyond themselves to solutions, to problems that might cost them or that might negatively impact their profitable understanding as public promoters of pedagogy. A New School would be independent of politics except for funding, having a blank slate for finding solutions to problems and would be immune to and not bent by interfering regulatory political pressure. The New School would benefit from meeting only educational needs for the good of the school, school staff and the students.

If the New School will ever emerge from a historically failed system, failed, but with honorable intentions, then its worthiness will be the result of the daily input of teachers and local administrators without which no realistic learning community can be constructed and maintained. In school, authority must be defended by the law, prosecuted and written by prosecutions of school lawyers to gain the right to be a truly learning community. A worthy school must have the power to silence protest against the unification process within the school. The whims of student-individualism are not to be advanced over the favor of a developmental individualism and in recognition of the contribution made for group identity by members within a truly educational community. The New School would insure a truly democratic education where everyone is given the expectation of a full academic public education without limits and without the channeling of students to special vocational training programs in preference to hard academic coursework.

A system of rapid-response for problems, provided by the redoubt system described, is necessary to prevent the influx of relentless cultural onslaught. The school should be able to act unilaterally and proactively to prevent the possibility of any derailing of academic progress in the school. A better defense will prevent the necessity of trying to beg for addressing the higher-ups for each new threat to the school. Redoubts can be rapidly deployed as defenses instead of responding to uniform policy, securing rules and consequences after the fact. In the New School, the good of the school comes first and not the feasibility of correction determined by those who only brush against real in-school education. The more radical approach would require a willing remote administration, the possibility of which is exceedingly unlikely given the political nature of their selection process. There would be no one-size-fits-all motif, a district wide direction for all schools. A version of the New School that took only some of the recommendations might be a more doable and therefore a more probable path because of its more gradual change in policy and direction. The charter school program across the country opens up the possibility of a more localized approach to reconstruction; if it finds success, then the chances for a New School reconstruction are favored. To produce an authentic public school built from the ground up by the school itself would allow the dissolution of layers of reforms, time out of mind, that have layered on one another and have ultimately recapitulated failure.

A reconstructed academic school with appropriate redoubts to protect children in a learning institution is the answer to modern school failure. I would long to see all schools operating for the benefit of learning alone, every school in this country, in every city, town and independent school district. If the personal and political will of those in charge could melt under the heat of failure, then, although realistic expectations are remote, idealistic even insane, public education would finally come in to its own. In order for this dream to be realized, there must be a ground swell of resentment directed at ineffectual leadership, at any and all levels. There must be a movement to bring this nation to demand education for all promised in ideals with a broad learned community. This is required in order to finally produce a true pluralistic democracy. There must be a dedication to the ubiquitous educational advantage, the ideal of the school as an academic institution, education for education's sake first, then only later a separate application of knowledge to all walks and labors of life.

If the New School is ever to emerge from a historically failed system from, no doubt, honorable first light, it must have the daily input of teachers and local administrators and the authority to quell the rebellion of the young and bring them into a community which can allow an informed growth and development of the young authoritatively overseen by adults. It must be a school that can stand against the culture that would see it sink unable to construct and maintain a clear academic purpose. We must guide students to a civil understanding of their place among others in the academic school.

Conclusion

If a man lose his balance and immerse himself
in any trades or pleasures for their own sake,
he may be a good wheel or pin, but he is not
a cultivated man.

- Ralph Waldo Emerson, Essays

Public education is a discipline that needs to gain a realistic understanding of children and of their world. Education, seen without restriction, is the response to the authority of learning without ideology and dogma, both of which defy growth and progress. That progress is being undermined by the very problems which have arisen to destroy pubic education, modern education has failed to win the hearts and minds of students who have settled for minimalistic literacy and dropping out. Many students have seen beyond all the theoretical hype and have identified education as a gimmick for which only a small number of students will persist to attain a successful professional life and an appreciation of letters. Students see the school as a self-perpetuating institution that serves itself. Students continue to successfully challenged the ulterior motives of modern education and have considered a public education relatively unimportant to their adolescent whims.

A true democratic education has ceased to be the goal of public education, which is primarily concerned with parametric issues such as dubious test score numbers and the mechanical admixture of those of a diverse school community. To rekindle the vision of an academic school, there must be a school reconstruction, the construction of a New School. The present public school is struggling to stay afloat among the incessant waves of cultural attack arising from both the extra-educational community as well as from student-individualism within the school that continues to establish greater authority at the expense of exemplary academics and a true community of dedicated learners. Cowed by parents and other remote litigants, manipulated by politicos and responding to calls for social programs to be instigated through the school, the school has lost dedication to timeless knowledge and the ability to model citizenship on proven principles and values.

The student-individual, must be reclaimed for the learning community. Currently the student-individual is an actor, who, by adolescent whim, would have education replaced by the entertainment world which occupies the student-individual's thoughts when he or she is not consumed with rites of self-canonization. The message has been so well received that students are more likely to study the cultural ideology than ideas or ideals which have deep reasoned value from the ancient past. Although learning is more worthy, it is considered of less value than the commodified lives to which students are being seduced. The public, and many in remote administration, for that matter, do not clearly see the broader value of exemplary education as value that continues to enrich and inform throughout life. For most of our history, the majority of public school students have been educated to the culture and by the culture and its consideration of value. The effect has been more effectively, in fact, than the academic school which has struggled in its classrooms to offer an appreciation for learning for the sake of learning itself. Success in chosen professions, measured in pecuniary rewards, has become the overpowering, if not the singular purpose of education for most students. Learning is merely a way to raise one's income, as Thomas Carlyle put it: it is the "cash nexus." It has been a topic of the right and the left. Even Marx used the concept to define the relationships within a capitalistic society as capitalists use the cash nexus to measure the value of an education. Many parents and school officials believe that school has no other function than opening up opportunity for monetary success and fame.

In the social realm, the "nexus" for education is not a connection among students and school officials but the link between the ambitious and the cash. The civil benefits are altered to accommodate the scaffolding convened within the school curriculum and ultimately scaled for a climb to the top of the work world. Civility comes to mean succeeding, even at the expense of personal friendship and community. It has been only through a sort of passivity toward diversity that broad-based community has been attempted. The spread and serial replacement of social education programs is symptomatic of the acknowledgement of a failure of schools to promote a socially meaningful equality. The truth is that public education in America has never been able to reform education such that a true democratic plurality has resulted. In the name of diversity and tolerance, all reforms and legislations have failed. The ultimate failure can be seen in the proposal of hate crimes. Diversity, emphasized as profoundly educational in nature, has resulted in academic shallowness, and, what has come to be thought of as tolerance, has resulted in the loss of conviction for academic values and condescension in fearful bigotry, to wit, that some groups may suffer from an uneducable incapacity. Academic and social competency divined by a dubious pragmatic understanding of capacities and evaluated in the form of an extra-educational business model, has sent some students ahead while other lag behind for job training prophetically confirming predictions of lower expectations by school functionaries. The history of education tells us that education was the pragmatic arm of business and the body politic into which we injected immediate cultural panaceas envisioned to allay all social obstacles to democracy. It is based on this argument that pluralism has not happened in the schools and that by remote administration public education has failed to produce a true democratic school.

John Dewey felt that education was to expand into all areas of daily life through experimentation, empiricism, and finding pragmatic justification confident in the successful addressing of any problems that might arise. Instead the ideologues of pedagogy - school activists, theorists and reformers - took his ideas and applied them, expanded some and modified some to invoke a societal or individualistic understanding and developing a public school that they wanted and thought that America needed. Wave after wave of reforms served only to minimize the very academic and socializing purpose of school by the very programs which were going to open the doors to democracy and equal opportunity. The elites were skimmed from the top to provide leadership and the masses were left to labor. This formula for the school population has become the intent and the result of centuries of public education proceduralism.

The American public school has not shown flexibility of practice, in having not opened up to the prospects of the majority of students who have been directed ultimately to non-educative purpose. No matter the knee jerk remedies applied to cultural and academic problems in the school, the context of understanding remains the same. Classism in education, despite a generation of attempted change, has consistently resulted in the provision for dual pathways, to leadership or to labor, whether based on race, intimations of intellect, or the station in life to which one might be born, there has been a mantra that "not all children should go to college." This is considered a realistic view of natural limitations based on the testable present and is not usually considered discrimination. In effect, despite all that has been done to superficially improve the image of the truly democratic school, the same historical race and class issues from earlier times still persist. Although less discriminatory than that which has been historically practiced, public education is still unable to recognize and provide equally for all students.

A prime reason for an inability to teach all the students is that it is currently impossible to hold a child to endure the rigors of an exemplary education. For some these are unswerving expectations, for others there are no expectations at all. Some would run to the opportunity to learn, while others would run even harder away from education to those diversions that bring immediate, illusory, shallow and replaceable satisfactions. Without the greater sustainable choices in life offered by a good education, opportunities are drastically reduced for both the One who runs from learning and the society that is secondarily a benefactor or the holder of debt. Students are compromising their educational mandate by seeing school as merely a legal requirement, a place in which One must remain until legal requirements for attendance are removed by age, or those students who find education to be a hat trick whereby playing the academic game expertly qualifies One to pursue a profitable line of materialism. When students, of any ability and attitude, can be made responsible for a good education, when student-individuals are directed to look beyond self to also consider one's benefit to Others, maximize academic dedication and meld social wisdom with civility, then America, on the basis of this kind of student civility and with a can-do-anything academic background, can build a greater nation in which together citizens can improve the future lot of all. It is then that American can find its way to the top of the industrialized nations in student performance without contriving phony tests of proficiency.

One must conclude that either schools are to be given the power and authority to control student responsibility or school is to become a warehouse, a holding facility in which to retain student individuals until they reach the age of legal self-responsibility and can be released to stand as adults.

The progressive education movement set a dangerous precedent in relinquishing excessive authority to the child. When the focus of all life seems to be on the young, as it would appear today, when numbers divested of absolute meaning determine the direction a student may be given in their work life and thought life for a life time, when order is little more than a paper tiger, then education, so directed, must fail.

An exceptional education in a civilized arena is not only a privilege of the rich or the intelligentsia but for everyone in a free democratic society. All that can be done must be done to insure that all children get as much academic education as is possible for the adults they will be and the society that needs more than minimally educated citizens. To do this, educational failure, bureaucratic ineptitude, cultural diversion and radical individualism in student behavior and attitude all having been left uncheck must be controlled for the sake of the education of America's youth. We must gain a new vision of what public education could be and what it has been seduced into being. The failure of modern education to provide the academic training for all public school students has been raised on the tripartite error of radical and extreme student individualism, the detached reign of boards of education which have little to no first hand knowledge of individual schools but prescribe for all indiscriminately and a culture that has been allowed, even encouraged to infiltrate, the learning environment. To turn education around this triad of tyranny needs to be taken down and a New School raised in its place.